SINGING YET

New and Selected Poems

BOOKS BY STAN RICE

SINGING YET

New and Selected Poems
by STAN RICE

Chatto & Windus
LONDON

First published in the USA by Alfred A. Knopf 1992

1 3 5 7 9 10 8 6 4 2

Copyright © Stan Rice 1992

Stan Rice has asserted his right under the Copyright, Designs and
Patents Act 1988 to be identified as the author of this work.

First published in Great Britain in 1995 by
Chatto & Windus Ltd
Random House, 20 Vauxhall Bridge Road,
London SW1V 2SA

Random House Australia (Pty) Limited
20 Alfred Street, Milsons Point, Sydney
New South Wales 2061, Australia

Random House New Zealand Limited
18 Poland Road, Glenfield
Auckland 10, New Zealand

Random House South Africa (Pty) Limited
PO Box 337, Bergvlei, South Africa

Random House UK Limited Reg. No. 954009

A CIP catalogue record for this book
is available from the British Library

ISBN 0 7011 6230 9

Printed and bound in Great Britain by
Mackays of Chatham PLC, Chatham, Kent

FOR ANNE
AND
FOR HOWARD O'BRIEN
1917–1991

§ CONTENTS

WHITEBOY

I. *America*

II. *Life with Father*

III. *Poems*

SOME LAMB

I. *During*

II. *After*

BODY OF WORK

NEW POEMS (1983–1990)

CONTENTS

WHITEBOY

1. *America*

§ ELEGY

1.

All life
      has song. Tho the ear be sad
still it sings songs.
Men cannot be so gone.

2.

Tell it
in rhythmic
continuity.
Detail by detail
the living creatures.
Tell it
as must, the rhythm
solid in the shape.
Woman. Arms lifted. Shadow eater.

3.

This may be paradise I do not know
anything is possible does not the rose bloom?
      Do not some flowers
        eat meat? Do they not smell like rotted rat?
        Do they not still glide through God's mind fluidly
without rancor? Ack-ack
        crackles in air. Snowflake is structured. Death
        stoops to pick up
Bleeding Thing. This may
      be
Paradise. At the least
          it is new.

4.

and/or
audit shriek of wrecking ball
  four stories of falling telephone calls, fifty years
  Hello, Goodbye, all that Talk. We dial

ROSEBUD or POPCORN and the lady answers and gives us

Time. O lord O vicious lord eating the black decimals
we are naked in our pyjamas on the back porch drinking sweet
wine at 5 a.m. the east gets pink the birds sing.

5.

And after Jackson's Bar toilet
lay down in sweet grass by highway
just to think
and got taken by unexpectedly clear pulse
that maybe was my own heart in my ear
but seemed to be in the ground
a heart without limits
in the ground
vomited and heard thought-contoured locomotive-whistle
towards Dallas.
No joy is merely a handhold on something less.
What it squeezes, it is.

6.

Joy will do. Woe you know.

7.

Pipe propped against Indian scraper-rock
dog snoring on couch
Anne asleep in moonlight-colored TV hisstling its dots

>   the movie over
Moon rising over Harold's house
parrot on perch conked by fate
The stunned charmed block
>   at 2.

8.

With old Japanese discuss
whether godly sperm leaps from silkworm
if one ignores the ritual of details; that is
rack, comb, heat, fingers, intelligence & passionate skill.
He assures me Not Possible.
And I say, What of excess, yeah, what about EXCESS?
And he says, Anything is easy before breakfast.
The idea being
to make the borders so far off they can no longer be called
The Border.

9.

It's easy to die she said it's always in you you give
in to it as tho It were a solo
you let It occur It is our finest power
Ive done It frequently she said
you just say, Calyx let that part
flower and at once such mangled tide of color comes
nothing feels incoherent and that which was sad
yields to the feeling of something you couldnt figure
the ending of ending exquisitely.

10.

At 28 I stop being 11: ripped cellophane

off the boy
the man at the microphone (or the woman) says
"This is the crackle of artifice artificially burning."
Radio

wrestles with air.
The pear dies twice. Once in memory.
Oleo angel opens
six-foot wingspread on the previous whiteness.

11.

What wants my mind—
rosebush? lawnchair?
Take.
Last night saw stars
between wires.
Ten of them, a long thorn.
Moon rises. Lawnchair
& rosebush maw
for mind's eye.

12.

Filthy kitchen, filthy bath,
filthy rug, I give my daughter a hug
and off we go, Peach and Fat
over the street to the beach
where the wind blows the waves back,
two kissers eating weenies, escaping house
in white Chevy borrowed for this
adventure, long tall Daddy and plump Mouse,
filthy hospital, filthy waves,
filthy wedding, filthy grave.

13.

No shit two days, no shit.
Cat warms by glass, fly-killing. Psssshhh
of machine, grinder or sawer or steamer.
In construction site guard dog's meaningless howl
echoes through naked rooms, not even
electricity to protect.
Rose withers in pot. Dwarf tangerines have actually shrunk.
The Oriental circle grinds
but causality is also beautiful.

14.

Matisse painted the philodendrons
fleshier than philodendrons are

and put amidst that symmetry goatmen playing flutes
and deer with shy turned necks, as tho drinking themselves.

That's how life feels
not how it is
how it feels.

For example, the lion that is eating the gypsy's dream
in Rousseau's painting

eats us all.

15.

Cry not, my baby.
Cry.
I know a frog ate a white moth.
The frog did not cry.
That's why he's a frog.
The moth did not cry.
Now moth is not.

My baby, cry not. Cry. There is much to do.
I will cry too.
We will cry for you.

16.

My cow; my past; my ripped song.
All one imagined WHOMP.
Lie down, lie down, you *are* a good person,
you do not diminish life,
you will have a wife who loves and in whom you are held
tight, till
WHOMP WHOMP
both as cows you are led
into a chute and hit.
Then we were married.
A snapshot of us outside our first apartment:
cow? why a cow?
Bowed in wet field, leaving her water-shelter
comes down hill each hoofprint
darkspots
the crushed dew. My past. Or: ripped song resembles
WHOMP-voiced
night. I sang It. It sang back: moo; more salt;
more green grass; leap me;
my spoon is greasy;
my cat fiddles with me;
mooing and making mooing and making.
Then we were married.
White, white the cow
with delicate legs,
snapped in place, aluminum yolk of milking machine,
the rubber nipples affixed,
pulsegush in can.
We bend over to be sent.
We straighten & brush off & walk
impersonating animals indifferent to Time,
shimmeringly indifferent. Mooing
delicately white-legged ventriloquists

chomp chomp
WHOMP WHOMP
Then we were married.

17.

Brushing her hair,
     the browngold strands
stick to the brush, rise—

the monster created by doing
the Clear Deed—.

18.

Sweet old woman dead with flute in brain
and husband's collection of highclass erotica
piled on tables & toiletbacks
out in the yard
a 50 year old pine planted by her she said
the dachshund bit its top off when it was a seedling
and I stared at it enrapt while beside me
passed Invisibleness quivering economical & swift
a light rain fell we built a fire but the flue
was closed the whole house filled with
love. Love is what you do. Pressed her body
lengthwise as he tied her cape, she smiled.
Sent him a note on leaving: Dear Sir, you were most
generous with an old lady out of prime.

19.

Hurting myself. Near nothing. 5 a.m. A glass of wine
chill fog first cigarette where are the saints?
Small sweetnesses
draw knives. Bird beak bird eye.
The black dot is wet. Is no solace.

And the arrows had stiff feathers
And they shot him with small sweetnesses
that he might hang hog
upside down, thick drops of paint-blood falling,
his speechbubble
pierced. East pinkens.
Streetlights on hills go off
dot dot dot go back in mood
and wait. Birds sing. 5 a.m. Sweet wine at window.
You have the vision you have the insight you cannot
survive them
not sober. Birds. Arrow-hogs. Not sober
see friend John in constant meanwhile
tied to the stake they cant light it his tears keep it wet.
Genius Guitarist Found
in Park, dew falling on dead face.
The newspaper documents the falling of the leaves
and he said, I read in the newspaper that the saints
are falling like leaves do you have a waterpipe?
I filled it with clean water.
The pain said Play the drum till your hands bleed
here's some tape play the drum. Lost,
all my friends, priests of risk, sleeping
on cutting boards, singing:
Alleluja Alleluja
If I bleed I must exist
Only hanging hogs get kissed
Only in the Hanging Dead
Do the words run to their heads.

20.

Much moon. Shadow eater woman
in bed, arms lifted, raised their length . . .
much black eyes closed
much morgue
moonlight on olive cheek.
And Durer gasped on first seeing Inca sun
six foot wide gasped silver moon . . . perceiving all men

had Craft & Giant Heart & who is savagery? Lost,
my friends, they took the metaphors literally, lost
in ramshackle moonlight kicking meat
the bus pulls up they stand in its headlights
the 7-Eleven manager cries out MUCH MUCH MUCH
my business is ruined . . . ketchup, all the ketchup broken . . .
the ice cream . . . the cola box turned over
you cant tell the ice from the glass . . . they didnt want
to *eat* anything they just wanted to *have* everything . . .
linoleum knife, dogchain, much much beauty
cut up. And Durer gasped at the ingenuity of man
and lay down to sleep with *that*
CHOMP CHOMP
his shadow ate him.

   21.

You laugh.
I do not laugh.

I am Tex Ritter. I am not Eldridge Cleaver.
I am approaching Havana.
I am carrying a pillow into the cockpit on which is embroidered
I am Tex Ritter. Howdy.
A calm falls over the cockpit.
The co-pilot takes off his extra ears and I tell them,
Relax. I tell the captain to tell the passengers
That this is not Eldridge Cleaver
this is Tex Ritter talkin
and we're going to Havana
and Relax. Then I hear the neighbor's black son's Pontiac
roar outside my window. I partly wake up. I look out.
He is wiping the water off the windows. Like a beast
out of the dream I just finished about living on a cliff
guarded by two white dogs with long flexible noses,
the Pontiac sits, its exhaust smoke
turns pink in the brakelights.
Does he know I am Tex Ritter? Does he realize
we have set down in Cuba, all of us, shrieking tires,
aluminum skin shuddering and windshield wipers
ferociously lapping the windows, the Cubans standing
behind the frosty reception room glass,
clipboards hanging from their belts, does he?
I'll bet he doesn't know.
I think I'll tell him.
But when I look back he and his Pontiac are gone. Oh well,
what's a skin-deep defeat to me, Tex Ritter?
Maybe it's better nobody knows who's talkin
when I kick in the cockpit door
and catch the pilots with their long soft black flexible noses
coiled in their laps, and slip
out of my embroidered pillow my gun and say, coolly,
We are going to Havana,
this is Tex Ritter,
this is not Eldridge Cleaver,
We are going to Havana forever!

§ UP AGAINST THE WALL

He kissed me on the mouth
in Dino & Carl's. Not sweetmeat of the female mind.
I said with my gestures,
"Charles, not all the shrieking boys in Tangiers
could make me do to women
what you ask of me."
And that ended it.
I felt my eyes become Eyes.

The etc
is the error. And in that error
shamed shape stood up from its barstool
and screamed: "God damn you why is it such a fucking
privilege just to see you!"
And a humm went over the still mothers-of-gloves.

I'll tell you why
men tingle.
Nothing is worth that much death
so soon.
It'd be better to be piled
shiny & akimbo
like squid in a tray
than suffer without succor.
A male bone was the first woman anyway.
Therefore he takes it in the mouth.
Sad substance weeping at the root of a pillow.
Feathers for fathers.

So I said to him, Charles "All that's increased by what you
        tell me
is the very vanity that keeps me remote
from your advances." Doom quailed behind his swimming glasses.
And, "Charles, porridge & poontang make the galaxy sway. Not your
hard-on on hard."
He let his head tilt on drunk neck.
It was at this point that he took me in his wilting arms
and lips.

§ FOURTH OF JULY IN THE RICH MAN'S HOUSE

1.

I sat in the fashionable supermarket of arteries
eating watermelon and assessing my merits.
Fireworks burst over the water.
Fused fire
and reflected fire. A white rocket pierced a green one.
Is Blake dead? The dead die.
Sausalito and London
meld in the strenuous liquor
of the watermelon twilight of fireworks over the black water.

2.

What is dancing
for, Mable? Use your imagination.
I wrap you in a snakeskin.
I put the bleeding bunting
in it. Mable. Fire is in the bloodcells. Mostly
your intelligence is electricity.
Mable. Ice is death ok. Writhe with me
across the parquet. Sweet are the muscles.
The silk whistles, and moisture is the mother ok.
Mable. Stretch. Begin.
The Fourth of July isnt under your skin with a needle
nor this snakeskin:
strips of membrane in talkative jelly.

3.

Courage
is the watermelon twilight's entities dividing
like melons on drainboards, the wet halves rocking
aside the cleaver.
This is what you do with your hips,
Mable.
This is what articulates the evening: total conceptualization

while opening the refrigerator—
the artificial twilight, the contours, the tomatoes, the peppers
erect, the milk,
the erotic.
This is it. Mable.
Hold me. Wrap the rinds in newspaper.
Have courage. Have an apple. Have my baby.

The logarithm. The fraction. The bead of dew.
The illusion. The quality
that leaps out of the bicycle. The possibility again
of heroism. The dispelling of sadness. The dynamo
and the huge act. The inclusion of machines
and therefore the mastery of machines.
The Big Dipper and the smoothness of aluminum.
The absolute colors. The April
that ascends and descends at once in the mercury.
The white bicycle of thought.
The way out of the doldrums of locomotives
and the smokestacks whose bodies are totems
of maniacal clarity. The moon
absorbed by the intelligence. All "property"
transformed without being "owned." The possibility again
of the heroic and gloomless claritas of sense.
Stoned visions of facts themselves.
The actual objects, around whose shapes accumulate the halos
         of presence.
The milkman come back, more jangling than war, the New War
declared on demythologized THINGS.
The investment of stone again
with the mercurial feathers and eyes
of the boneless breeze.
No victory but in the perception of the emotional quality.
Victim and victor transposed. The melting down
of the locomotive in the machine of its making.
All rhythms seen as extensions of spirit.
All spirit seen as extension of motion.
The ferociously benevolent dilation of the eye
at the warcraft of Knowledge. At last
the vision complete of this: that the excesses of today
are the natural resources of tomorrow. By which
the data quivers with delight in the graph,
and the formerly dead hairdomes ignite with feeling,
and the moosehuge inanity of literal competition
is transformed into the ecstatic sexual come.
Not the loss of all energy into sloth
but the internalized energy of sensual synapses,
of galaxy and water and brilliant brain and breast and nipples

and scrotum and mons and scarlet tip.
America The Beautiful. At last
the Constitution made fact and the fear of actualized Liberty
renounced and the Void smoothed like a bed.
I pledge allegiance again,
this time to the vivifications of our lost Body Politic,
nerves and follicles and arteries
ablaze in the suaveness of night.

§ *LOOKING AT THE MOON DURING THIRD MOONWALK*

1.

I write these words by Carmel Valley
moonlight. I write them large
as in a child's book. Lamb or calf
mews far off. Cars pass on road.
I write it down amazed
at the size of the Tabula
Rasa.

2.

Debris is full of design.
Time is duration.
I try to see the three-dimensionality of the stars
but all I can see is Cathedral Dome, dots in the dark.
        I make
this life. It does not flood, like Time, the body. Joy is a choice.

3.

came back from language Whole.
earth shies. our shepherds are robots.
shapes drip on moonlit lawn
by swimmingpool. I ignore my responsibilities:
                humanitas
                claritas
                sensualized intelligence.
            blobs of light
        wobble in
That Which Is.

4.

Immorality is the repression of potential.
Shepherds, tending little blobs,

tend your shapes.
Luna was soft, a lover of men. She's dead.
Venus bled seas.
Drops of her menses shine on the golf course.
Black crow
bitches in
gleamy dusk.

5.

The man who massaged my feet
until I fell asleep
told me that as I slept
my face was in a beautiful repose
almost like death.

§ 3 A.M. OPENING THE WINDOW

Because I will die
I open the window
at 3 a.m. I am up writing
and drinking
and dying.

In the Yellow Sea
the South Koreans report
death never retreats,

nor from the Wailing Wall
do new deaths
step back blessed.

The night air
is cool and watery.
Lows in the 50's.
Highs in the 70's. Occasional drizzle.
Those are the facts, says the radio. But

we forget.
Right?
The North Koreans
report
the Yellow Sea
is sorry.

But we are drowning
and wailing.
In Lima
after The Earthquake
clean water
was gold.

It is death's
drizzle we write
checks on.

When we die
we bounce.

In the public toilets of the world
many of my friends find the everlastingly honest poetry
of graffiti, "only true literature
of the average heart." I find that too; but mostly
when I read those walls I read
the shy, sad language of men who are the voyeurs of their
    own lives.
And when I see those huge, well-drawn cocks and balls
(how rarely a well-drawn cunt, which of course
is harder to draw) I see
the self-piercing penis of death,
the weapon of a losing war,
the stark ink prick dripping its stylized teardrops of sperm,
and I am made sad,
sad for women,
sad for the men who fear women so fiercely in their hearts
that they must display to the world
of men
the size of their huge loss.

§ WHITEBOY

I.

The Texan reads a book.

Each night has new meaning
in it. Tonight. Aeschylus, I hear your black and gold mask
thunk in the yard, where each leaf of ivy
comes up
reaching and sparkling.

It's like a . . . like a . . . party:
the terror hosting the terror hosting
the tendrils. They are white,
their strength coils through the black yard like
a snake around a chicken egg
it swallows without breaking.
Gold souls in fragile things: Im watching the stars
in the black branches and Im thinking of the meaning
this man's death has.
If it will last.
If any.

It's April.
The guests in my garden
stick out their white tongues under the dirt.
Light gives them color.
It changes the complexion of the mask.
Aeschylus, I hear in my brain rather than in my ears
your deathmask clink against the gravel.
This night means I am in it
up to my lips. Kick Me.
I am beginning.

His head stuck up
because the hero is always more visible. Or rather,
he was a hero and therefore his head
stuck up above the sludge we call the flow we live in.
BANG!   Aeschylus, you said:
          God marks that man with watchful eyes
          Who counts his killed by companies;

And when his luck, his proud success,
Forgets the law of righteousness,
Then the dark Furies launch at length
A counter-blow to crush his strength
And cloud his brightness, till the dim
Pit of oblivion swallows him.

But this is not a Literary Poem.
I am aware that this is a Poem.
I am singing but I am sinking
into the little black hole
in Martin Luther King's black jaw.
Or, as one of his friends put it: "His face just exploded."
The language got too much.
His life stopped working.

So what is a dead Greek to this dead nigger?
At the Vice President's fund raising dinner where the news came
out the Chaplain said:
     "The-king-is-dead-long-live-the-king-of-peace-on-earth."
Meaning: each night has new meaning in it.
Meaning: we have heard that soft language before and it grew
          white ivy.
Meaning: I am. My black roots are hair. Are
showing.

        2.

The Texan sees the children with the crushed souls for the first time.

Suave children black and brown
stand in my ivy patch
knocking on the openings in bottles
with their palms.
Standing in the wide leaves
each still an ear of dew
making the bottles sound like
they are grief stricken. Children without real eyes
in their heads I think

standing in my ivy patch
if I struck their faces with my palms lightly
would thunk like bottles
so pure is their emptiness.

The physical world around them a mystery,
no little animals,
no yellow,
just holes in their faces.
Give them many bottles,
wet their lips with Coke,
suave black and brown bodies full of echoes,
scary as Death in the ivy standing
knee-deep in the green ivy,
beating on the mouths of bottles with their palms,
grieving and smiling.

3.

*The Texan returns to the Texas State Fair and sees Racism sitting in a
glass cage over a tank of water.*

And here is where the niggers wash.
You can kill a nigger at last.
You can throw a baseball at the target hooked to his body.
You can pay him back for his sensual blackness.
You can drown him and drown him but still
he will laugh like a sleek, stupid ape,
because that's what he is;
sleek; shiny; the whites of his eyes all yellow;
the brown pupils covered with a mucous blue film;
the teeth. You can make his seat snap open
and down into the white filthy water he drops,
his black hands and feet mixed in the foam,
staring at you through the glass tank
like an animal that you cant kill,
you cant kill him,
he keeps rising all oily and fresh, like a seal,
taunting you, virile, soiling you, soiled, your victim, your master.

4.

The Texan re-reads a book.

Agamemnon's slit jaw on the floor's Lord blooms
like a beautiful idea about freedom.
My-vacuumed-room-will-not-grow-ivy
April-to-it-is-merely-a-season
so WHAT?
So let the ears of ivy hear me
knock on my ears until the gunfire
forces a bloodred rain from the thunder.
Im sure that Agamemnon's golden deathmask is a fake.
Martin Luther King's skin is awake in my garden.
It talks.
It says: your uncle's, your father's, your brother's, your own
bones bones bones
are pale and rotten and crushed and swallowed.
The little black hole in his cheek
sprouts water. Tonight.
I see.
I am.
My own.
Skin's father.

The street is no river. For slouching
they put big rings of white lime
around each elm tree in the yard
outside the lunchroom. The Mexicans
are throwing switchblades at the locker room wall.
The grape-ade has flicked its cock.
In metalshop the whiteboy is running his twofoot
bread-knife along the buffing-wheel,
the soapstone melts; desire, alongside his leg, desire;
& outside, broad low-slung Chevys cruise
from the 7-Eleven to the freeway.
That wool in the woods is girl's wool.
Maybe them what eats shit set fire to the tires
stacked in the trees beside the Lighthouse
For The Blind. Or some jelly-bellied
cop searched everybody when Everybody
dropped cherrybombs down the toilets.
The excuses ran out on you, whiteboy. The flashlights
walked on invisible legs in the alleys.
The percentages got better of you getting it like Billy Bob
got it in a car wreck or like whatsisname, the one with all
    the hair,
shot in the throat, the rest of his life
proud of not being able to talk: Lovers of Knives. Well, shit, I
remember easy all the lives that ended at 16
because nobody loved love as much as the circular bone
    in the penis
that shows when youre backed up against
the white lime. Here come
the gringos Lefty & Carl, and then the Mexicans
Juvey & Moses & Menchaka, my life
flickering between fence slats between the woods of tires
and the miniature golf course, my small chest
shrinking even more, hair sleek with Fitches,
my percentages increasing with each evasion.
Whitey in black leather is whitey alongside
browny's suave Jesus, sterling silver
crucifix at the throat, suede & ancient, lies lies lies,

bilingual angels, jelly-handed murderers, arsonists,
big prick-mongers sliding down plaid seatcovers
into their own lives, somebody's gonna gitcha, razors
in boot toes, fear fear fear in beautiful eyes,
liquid as polish, endlessly flickering,
dogchains hanging out of the mouths & sides.

WHITEBOY

II. *Life with Father*

Jane was my jam.
The movement of fish
fleshed out her dress.
She could glide on one side like a dish.
When she had a wish the sun rose in her hair.
When she strolled by
swimming pools had tides.
Her poetry was the honest gesture.
She was imagery all in a line.

Leather bands
Trout
Northern bones
Thirteen eggs
Dishes of gravy
Fish winking
White arms
Girl-wet
contrivances to open oysters
Gestures meaning "sort of"
Seltzer
Black figs
Olive trees
Greece a penis in water
Travel to another climate
A tarantula in artificial light
An underwater photograph of a shark
Bread
Vulvas all in a row
A cradle of mirrors: truly

my jam was Jane. She kissed me beside the hamburger stand.
It was my signal to drive great distances.
To the drugstore. To her father's bed.
To the livingroom of a friend.
Jane my darling, my darling Jane.
Chicken-fryer, player of badminton,
upholsterer.

If there is a pure poetry without contrivance
then you are an ankle
and a salad, a hardness in lambskin.
And if the sun goes up and down and up and down
as naively as it seems to,
then you are the pure poetry of its disappearance
into the light black trees
by the liquor store.

Molasses without winter
Coming along anyway
Being in water
Having toothaches
Opening wine
Touching a stranger's hand by accident
Looking through a telescope
Necessary gestures
Laughter *during* a journey
Calmness when the border dissolves
Sugar in the night
Understanding women
Coming to terms
Being a man
Syrupy sun
Jane Jelly.

S *SONNET*

You throwed me away.
Someone else is bringing you your gum.
Im sorry for how I drove you against the sofa
with my words. They musta
hurt. Pings,
against your white arms.

There's a sleek underground
you shoulda ripped
the Christian veil off of. But that's that.
I was blind.
Was it Juicy Fruit?
I smelled you in my car for weeks, over by the window.

The rain fell. It was our Carnival Date.
They let down the wagon-shutters.
The hammer game glowed in the air. He guessed my weight.
My muscles went home with the stripper.
It was your fault. Until those last two lines

this was a sonnet.

§ THE PROPOSITION

Are you telling me the truth?
If I go up to your room
how can I do anything else? It is a mystery.
I look into your eyes
on the street, among all these strangers.
I see a fear.
The fear is in your eyes and also on your face.

So I go with you
and every stairstep I hate myself more for how I am using you.
The truth should have come first.
Your bed is not made.
Your pillow is on the floor beside the bed.
When you take off your blouse
my mouth goes dry, as when handling a harmless snake.

I know I will pay and pay.
But what is worth it, unsquandered?
Will I be reincarnated brave and rich?
No I wont be reincarnated brave and rich.
So I pull your pants down
and my heart beats so hard I am afraid
you are smiling at me, up there.

When I am through with you I realize
it is you have used me, I am the one
the fear ate. Change nothing
in this moment except what we feel about each other.
If asked again
I would come up to your room knowing this humiliation
is not the only sleep you give me.

I wait in the cafe for my wife like a gorilla
promoted to pull a red wagon
with a blond in it
through the Circus.

It's raining.

The rain thumps on the awning.

Paranoia takes the shape of a vulture
washing down its dinner
of tourists. The Gray Line Bus
passes. They disboard. They run into the red lobby.
Anne is late.
My watch quacks in my pocket.

The vulture lifts its clean beak.
Its neck a shining intestine.

I open a book of translations
and flutter the pages
and stop on
these words: *moths*
crackling like sugar underfoot.

In the drugstore on the corner
a sequence of flashbulbs goes off.
Then a woman's laughter,
like at an unbelievable threat to her body.

A maroon limousine stops at the light. The chauffeur
wears a black cap and his passenger
is the color of paper. An umbrella's
hook at her cheek. From the waist up
she is a lamp, a table lamp.
It moves past.

Anne is late again. Nearby,
a yellow newspaper rack. I can read
the headline. It says:
TROOP CUTBACK HINTED. Above the fold
there is a photograph of a blond in a swimming suit
astride an enormous turtle.
A newspaper left on the table behind me

blows up. Giant paper heart
attacks my chair.

Inside, the bartender polishes glasses.
His cummerbund is on his shoulder.
I flutter the pages to this:

Green laurel lives on in the kitchen,
the voice doesn't change.
What does that mean?
I read it again, in context. "Dora Markus," 1939, Montale.
It is a pretty picture. I get an insight:
Love of the grotesque begins with fear of the body.

Christ's blood. Picasso. Rimbaud. Enrapture.
Anne, where are you?

The bartender is putting the chairs on the tables.

§ FORGETTING HER BIRTHDAY

Yesterday was her birthday
and I simply lay with her birthday

and I simply used her birthday
and turned once in the night

without making a wish
and blew out her hair.

She dreams the dream of the washing machine.
It overflows.
I dream the dream of the burning paper.
It climbs my fence.
My fence is no barrier.
A boy with big shoes jumps into the fire-pit
out of fear. The white sheets curl up
in the bricks. The laundry
rises and falls on the floor
of the porch. We were together asleep.
She watches the overflow rise.
I watch the paper, the burning sheets rise,
rise up, rise up the bloodstained handkerchiefs.
Then we wake up.
Her washing machine purrs and the lid is closed
and its whiteness purrs.
My burning-paper dream becomes a dirt yard.
We lie in the white bed.
There is an argument welling.
We can both feel the incomplete resolution of rising garbage.

§ STORMING OUT

She goes out into the cold night
to search for the She
with the guts.
Death is firmest where it is fluid.
A bucket rises with my body in it.
She looks in it and says, Well, there you are,
chopped up in little pieces, and sure enough,
no guts either.

§ POEMS AND MARRIAGE

I think my roots are growing
down through this chair
and not into my marriage.
A vain and selfish flower
with combed leaves
is growing downward from my
tip-of-spine. One day
standing up from this chair
will rip my heart out.

Get lost, she said.
She did not have to give such good advice
Twice.
I left.

Or, I got *lost.*
What light!
Until I wasnt anywhere
I didnt know where I was.

I came back
And said,
Here I am.
Who are you?
She asked.

I dont know anymore,
I sighed.
Good, she said,
Then come inside.

Inside it was
wide and weird.
She clung and whispered,
What shall I do?
I whispered,

Disappear.
I did not have to give such good advice
Twice.
Goodbye! she shouted.
And drew near.

The queen is in the sifter.
Trapped by the silver hoop, she stares up, doubled
black and yellow. The king
is in the strainer. Jacks
on the white leaf
of the table.
We are the bridge builders.
And the gorge is health-honey.
Spade heart clubs diamond.
We are making News, killing Time.
I trump your roast leg of lamb.
You turn my queen's red handle.

§ FIRST XMAS AFTER DAUGHTERDEATH

1972

Christmas Day . . .
The Morning Star closes its lips in the gum trees . . .
My niece turns the handle of the pencil sharpener . . .
Her cinnamon-roll shines in the sun . . .
Where the gnats fly.

Now theyre gone to her Grandmother's . . .
The candles stick up their wicks . . .
The coffee can full of pot; ah! he left it . . .
The rubber head of the rooster-puppet continuously crowing . . .
Yet things are not ok.

In a deep lake gloom not of my making . . .
Pressure in the head . . .
Playing with my niece, beside whom milk would look yellow . . .
Growing my beard so that my face will look fatter . . .
Where death holds me by the ankles.

Dont look backwards the blackness will blind you . . .
Christmas . . .
The unbought trees lying on their sides by the Bank . . .
Anne wakes up walks in opens a beer stares at the window . . .
We dont speak.

WHITEBOY

III. *Poems*

S SONG

The birds do not sing. The whales
do not sing. Their sounds are painfully urgent: like talk.
In hysterical restraint
apples fill the tree we call
the Apple Tree, and drunks watch
the severed intelligence of their quivering hands
in awe. It is not to sing that we speak
but to speak that we sing. More than we know.
The pure, the merely pure song is hollow.
Even the whale speaks. The drunk sings on.
His words have the contour of song
but it is language he longs
to sing. What the bird sings is *bird*. Words
are things.

Once we had the words.
Ox and Falcon. Plow.
There was clarity.
Savage as horns
curved.
We lived in stone rooms.
We hung our hair out the windows and up it climbed the men.
A garden behind the ears, the curls.
On each hill a king
of that hill. At night the threads were pulled out
of the tapestries. The unravelled men screamed.
All moons revealed. We had the words.
They liked us.
Then we lost them.
They fell out of love with the things they called
"ox" and "falcon." Plows
lay tongue-out in water. The hills lay down.
The gardens. We cleared them. We listened.
The men climbed down our hair
and rode off on horses.

Be with me now
my husband.
At night the birds call me
to go out on the porch
dressed like this,
my hand squeezing the collar.
Impossible slowness of what we want.
Charles! I cry now
every yard is of birds, the lizards
slithering over the windows
are my wedding bands,
and the rain pours from the roof
when I lie down on this bed
of needles without you.

She is going to die.
She is going to gracefully
go lie down alone
as she lived, as
the elephants.
Lay down the light teeth. Ears. In fact,
the children.
Whatever room she is in
Death stands in
red pumps
at the doorway.
He is also a Lady.
Every edge fits. The world is all function
come to nothing. Womb,
once apulse, now neither loved nor hated
she looks out and feels
pure function
a monster. Death
at the door
in red stockings.

§ I RIDE THE FLYING PIG

merry-go-round, 1969

I ride the flying pig!
His ears stick up with excitement!
His eyes look out at the galaxy!
They do not see me!
He has two fangs that come up over his lips!
He does not feel the brass pole in his back!
He wears a purple saddle!
I ride him through the mirrors!
The flying pig does not feel me!
I am as light as his saddle!
He has no reins!
The sunlight falls on the white benches!
The pig flies over the gleaming benches!
The brown eyes never change!
He is the flying pig with courage!
No rider can alter his cruel expression!
His little hooves stick out in front and in back!
He glides over the wood!
No one is as beautiful as my flying pig!
Not even the flying lion and the flying jackrabbit behind us!

I.

Tree-bud
stars on concrete. Hosed off
they lie
mixed
in gleam-mud.

2.

A firetruck passes, wiping my room red.
Everybody comes out into the street, in t-shirts, arms folded,
pretending not to be too curious. It's a false alarm.
The firemen stand on the truck in their black slickers
looking around. The dogs are excited.
Then what makes a crowd congeal
dissolves, the petals fall off, the t-shirts
blow away.

3.

What's "natural"?
        Are the girls in their transparent dresses
bending over the drinking hydrant
        natural?
A man approaches me with waxed walrus moustache.
        Is dancing?

4.

The sugarstiffened stems
                under the shading pine
ooze. Wasps whirr in the needles.
                Dew dries.
Avalanche calm   crushes human watcher.

SOME LAMB

I. During

My mother groan'd, my father wept;
Into the dangerous world I leapt,
Helpless, naked, piping loud,
Like a fiend hid in a cloud.

WM. BLAKE

§ PLAYING IN THE YARD

I.

Green daddies
      can. Apples in the dustpan.
Birds in the feeder
      eat. They know. Each spring daddies lost.
The dog growls at the wall.
Apples roll. It's the law.
The dog kills the bowl.
The leash has friends.
The apple is in my clothes.
      One end loves hair and
      one end loves bones.

2.

Big chocolate. Milk cup. Bread.
More toys. Daddy
more water. Star. Two stars. More two stars.
I walk. I run. I run.
Stay in bed. I stay in bed. Three mirrors
talk talk talk.
I watch News. Two news.
I walk chocolate. I run. Run stars. Stars run.
More stars walk my news. My bike walks.
My bed talks stars.
Big
dog.

3.

The Book Of The Children.
It told where the weather came from.
The clouds with voices.
The buckets of rain passing down the fire-line of children.
The fire at the end of the book.
The four-legged thunder.
Lightning

Quick-Runner
Hurricane. Hurry, Cain.
Torn Tomato. Tornado. Snow. Sleet's
white teeth
fall from the mouths of the children.
The fire in their curled hair.
The Book Of The Children.

4.

The grass drinks milk.
    It's ok.
The grass drinks milk.
Here comes the black dog
    we don't love.
An all black dog and an all white dog.
Oh-kay. Oh-kay. Let
the leash come.
They eat sleep.
Sleep eats them.
Dogs are warm.
    We love
putting the lemon in the purse.
    We have arms.
Green is our guard. Some nights are white,
    some.
Sticks live in trees. Here come
the rocks. The apples come
in fall. Leashes know
    our motto:
kiss my claw
white dog.

I.

Five smooth piggies went to town
to buy smooth gowns
to wear to the Grand Ball
to be held in the bleeding Fall.
Five gowns they bought
of smooth cloth and five bone pins
and twenty cloven shoes
of pigskin.

2.

The lambs went out with little tails
and came back without them.
The tails are dripping from a bough
and dare you shake them.

3.

Strawberries and sugar and cream
Goldilocks feeds
herself and sews
a fine seam in the hem
of her gown silver and rose
until a black rooster pecks
to get in her clothes
and his cruel truth crows.

4.

The father of the lambs
is leaping in the pale
water where his naked daughter
shears him with her fingernails.

5.

> I cannot see
> *through* my eyes
> the ram that licks
> the garden dry.

Daughter, asleep in the back of the house.
A cat cries in heat. You wake. Red
as blood your cheeks.
From now on call every cry
Daddy. Who died?
The trees.
The blown leaves gather at the fence.
You start scream's water, Child. We are the same
    nearly.
Sighs crushes pressures.
Tomorrow, I'll skin that scream in the sink.
Close your round eyes,
Roundeyes.

§ FOUND

She asks me if I will keep the kitten she has found.
But I know

that as it develops
form will devour it,   I say

Well, it's a problem.   And she
says,

No, I just found it this morning   last night
it wasn't born.

§ DYING GOLDFISH

He takes death hard, my goldfish.
He does not see it orientally,
As a continuity.
He resists like crazy.
It's been three days.
The children have already made him a grave
Of daisies and dirt in an orange bowl.
Every morning they come in to check.
Last night my daughter woke with leukemia pain
And I went in to find out what was wrong and she said
Is my fish dead yet?

§ SURVIVING

Tongue and talk
We survive. The mouth on the couch backstage
Next to the stoned dumb mirror
Nailed by the lightcage
We survive.
Even the source. Even the TV in the empty ballroom
And the toilet brightness that survives by dying
And the cadillac star in the parking lot
That won't extinguish
We survive.
Even Death's crushed ice eyes and beer barrel pupils.
Tongue in the mouth, mouth of the mask, mask on the one
Who survives.

§ HOMECOMING

Here sits the man
Who wrote some poems and visited the Dugong
In the Moonlight Clay Pan
& drank lots of THAT
& whose name means Stone
Field In Which Nothing Will Grow.
Here he sits writing
Wishing he were at the Moonlight Clay Pan
Dugong with a lady whose big eyes stare down out of skin.
Here sits the man after six days
In his motionless oceanliner Hospital
Writing on his machine fast as fast can.
Here comes the cigarette to his lips and the green flash of the match
And the next beer.
And here's his eyeflash at the pan of needles
Each in its own wrapper like a witch's gland
When he took his child in for her checkup
And they kept her and put a tube in her wrist
And a strip of witch's skin over her hand.
Here's his dog Daisy in heat
Leaking on the couch, and here's his wife Anne
Shampooing the carpet.
And here is the poem he wrote on his machine
While home for a couple of hours,
Happy, very happy, like you'd be in a war
When you've made it from one place to another
And no bomb has fallen on your head.

§ THE 29TH MONTH

A thing, loved one,
is eating our air.
It dwelleth in oily hair.
It dwelleth in the chair by the window.
It dwelleth in the lying-out-white baby.
A man enters in a smock
and it isn't the cook it's the doctor.
What's up, Doc?
He says the medicines can make her sing but can't make her talk.
So we bought her twenty-five dollars' worth of chocolate eggs
whose shells melt and centers flood and the days,
ah,
the days,
they move so slowly,
people come in and out of the parkinglot carrying zinnias,
the dentist in the window leans over his oven,
the gardener waters the concrete,
little black girls in green crinoline come to visit their grandfathers.
The body doesn't lie.
I want to make it be in words, because
to get the poem right
is to have another baby
while the real one dies.

The Substance Beast is very cruel.
It plants me in the oil school.
It beats my knuckles with a stool.
I'm chained to it like fists to fools.
I wish I could be like Michele Fair,
Who dug her grave in her yellow hair
And took off her clothes and stood there
Waiting for the Beauty Bird.
She hummed and murmured I Don't Care
When the truant officer cut her hair
Off with a set of silver tools.
But the Substance Beast keeps check on me
To see that I have fed it me
Just as policemen like to see
A proper show of humility in those they rule.
Someday maybe I'll be like Michele, free-flowing
Baldness, at night regrowing the yellow hair
That covers the grave she's dug to snare
The Beauty Bird, the Naked Knowing.

In the twenty-ninth year
My mind matured
To the point that I could hear
Sounds and see things as though
They were visions.
The occasion, death.
If like people it took breath
Or as leaves the stones exhaled water
That was important
And meaningless. I began to include
The insights on Acid. By those truths
Lies became as useful as those absolutes
I once thought I could never smile at
Compassionately.
My capacity for belief increased
As my number of beliefs diminished.
Finally the trees popped
Or were cannibalized
And I sat down drunk on the curb
With my feet ankle-deep in the petals
That blew up and gathered there.
Two years earlier on hearing
The diagnosis was leukemia I lay down
On the linoleum and saw a door shut
On what *is*. The distinction between that
And hallucination became irrelevant.
The nervous doctor was an oil painting.
When I walked outside
The plants in the sunlight
Were extremely vivid
And the people walking
In and out of Woolworth's
Were as clear as angels
In an icon. Only two choices
To stress: go on, or give in.
Nothing made sense but each entity's
Hunger to be what it is
And to thrive until it suffers
The heart attack of the ice cake
Or carnation, the two speeds. I walked

Through the people and saw
They were like freshborn animals
Before they can open their eyes
To discover that the source
Of the milk of kindness
Is always moving.
Nothing mattered therefore
But the ambivalence of accurate
Illusions: art.
I saw that Events had
Emotional skeletons
And that the worms could be lured
Out of substance
And that Thoughts had the sad
Psychological flesh
Of things with faces.
Two years have passed.
I care so much
I don't care any more.
Hello hello.
Goodbye goodbye.

What's that red stuff? Blood? Gee
ZUZ! Go down on THAT,
Baby-eater.
So? The pillow has fangs. So?
Something's too soft here.
OK, tell me: what does an angel's skeleton look like?
Looks like the shadow of a bunch of chains.
Jesus. I'm sitting up all night with a fern.
I'd cry but my eyes got eaten by . . . uh, who was that anyway
Ate my eyes? Some "god"?
He got hungry and he needed some silverware so he opened
My daughter and he said, Look at this here little faceful of bones:
FORKS & KNIVES & SPOONS & BUTTERKNIVES.
God, bruise-stomper, purple to puss, crusher of children,
Beerbelly, tattoo on bicep reading YUM YUM
In a valentine being squeezed by a chain
& a vulva with a lightning bolt in its eye.
Zero with teeth, leukemia-licker, slut.
It IS blood, that red stuff. GEE
ZUZ! Somebody dropped the watermelon on the concrete.
Get a sponge. Get a shovel. Call God. Soup's on.

1.

Looking up at the stars, connecting the dots.
From the dayroom
A ghosthole TV illuminates
Kerouac's fine poem
"The Thrashing Doves."
The nurses are playing cards . . . laughing.
It's all very simple.
Thought moves in meat.
Meat moves in thought.
We see puzzles
Where only stars are.

2.

In the sun the muscles are gardens
Of creamed-style corn
And lightning bolts.
In this hospital courtyard
Ditto. Stars
Pinpoint the vast gristle
And nothing of WHAT.
If we were statues we would fear earthquakes.
Since we aren't we fear everything.

Everything she drank
Turned to blood, even the turned
       shadow of her face, blessed
Contour, immeasurably
     exact, patient, painting,
Turned to blood
In the end. Hummingbirds & snails
     in shadowdrinking flowers
So red they were pale,
  so complicated at the end
Everything she said
Turned to blood, every word,
   the ghost-petal TV cow,
   the shadow of a waterglass,
    everything she saw
Turned profile to her
    and the blood stopped,
The machine showed so,
       the crushed ice she was eating
Turned to blood.

§ INCANTO

I.

I sit waiting for one of the two kinds of miracle:
the thing as it *is,* or the thing *transformed*—
which Tyger?—
There are no lambs here, my juicy head—Time
hath made off with the last lamb left—That's dead—
Anne sits reading the Chronicle in her nightmare clothes—Daisy
glossy on couch—I hear a broom & a hose on concrete—my
    neighbor,
sweeping his reflection away, no doubt—The photographs are in the
    album
each face under its plastic, waiting, for the Real, the cheek
crushed to cheek
that the brain might arc the gulf between brains—Orgasm?—
A huge hand comes out of the clouds and squeezes the brain
and lets it go
and it soaks back up what it let—selfdrenched again—astonished,
a mirror in grass—
Is the miracle *clarity?*—precise definitions instead of this *song?*—
Which tyger shall eat the reflection?—If I'm to go on
the terms of the slaughter must be known—
Hugeheaded child lying on couch beating her lace collar
under which is the pain in her lungs—
The precise names of the medicines
did not help:
6-mercaptopurine prednisone cytoxin methotrexate dilantin
thioguanine vincristine asparaginase cytocine-arabanacide
        NO HELP—
At 4 a.m. I wake up on hospital linoleum beside her bed TV
hissing the screen a miracle of chaos not a single word
worth saving they're all too small throw them back no limit
to errors the faces are under the plastic in the album two
months have passed she's dead that's it the scissors lie in
the moonlight on the bedstand clarity is cannibalism—
Sunday—8 October—72
Michele now nothing but an emptying dress in the grave.

2.

White day—glare—light on the liars—
Outside the Rainbow Carwash & Lounge
the blacks in ankle-length leather—shoes of shame vanished—
lightning in leather—All the names of the colors
in the 48 count box of crayolas,
listed—Clarity & Vividness joined—screamy with silky—
The books articulate, intact—poodles barking at windows—a girl
at a curtain, reading—a white dress drying in a tree—
ruthless clockshop window & enameled scarlet chinese porcelain egg
    on crunchless velvet—
And not *one* human in the landscape who is not a metaphor—
Everything metaphor except the metaphors—Gesture is sculpture—
The swinger stands fixed in nitrogen
and the brain that talked just an hour ago shines in a jar—
To write this right is to cope with the corpse—
I kissed her in the coffin, the big cool rubber doll in the coffin,
she smelled like crayolas, her face
a Thought—
Hold on—even in heaven, frozen in gold—in the boneyard
where the clock coughs, hold on—in the marble, safe against seepage,
hold—in the dirt, in the neutral, hold on
that you might be able,
should the miracle come,
LET GO.

3.

I let her go, I told her, me, squeezing the oxygen bag,
Electrocardiogram ink line straight to horizon, no blip,
Precision useless again, Chief Doctor
In rumpled suit no tie unshaven 5 a.m. & fumbling Intern,
This probably his first death, mine too,
Anne in her blue robe astonished, after two years, still,
    at the last moment,
ASTONISHED,
Fingers to lips,

The oxygen tent ripped back, the cooler roaring for nothing, me
Squeezing the rubber bag trying to find the rhythm of a breather
    sleeping
That her heart might recognize, begin again, all the time
Saying to myself "Don't come back Mouse don't come back," her
    head
Heavy on rubbery neck the veins I'm ASTONISHED
Rising to the surface of the skin like crazed lacquer, One Two Three
Shots of adrenalin straight into the vein,
No response,
Me squeezing now the tears dropping bright on the black rubber bag
    No Response,
The head nurse massaging the chest a deep gurgle like a clogged trap
NO RESPONSE, Anne
"Can't we do anything, isn't there anything else we can *do?*" The
    Doctor
Stands up, "You can stop now, we might as well stop kidding
    ourselves, she's
Gone," and my head cocks sideways like the RCA Victor dog
& I bend over & her lips part easily & wetly & I give her
the long kept sexual kiss of father
to daughter, too late
Hello.

4.

Enough is never enough—That voice comes back—Suave shells of
    gesture
in doors—The photographs just holes full of crayolas, a glare
in a book—Never enough—Anne drinks, pregnant with novel, writes
    & screams—
Ten twelve fifteen beers, never enough—
Once more smallvoiced prophetess bald and swollen in final months
    in red
wheelchair spoke the truth & knew no other thing to say & Death
    ate her
& Death wasn't even hungry—Well,

"when the sun goes to sleep it makes a hole in its bed"—
There was no key to lock the door no emergency shriek no police the
    rapist
came in under the door a crack too small even for light to get
he got—Backwards, that—Forward, Michele as a model—Meanwhile,
the poem, for a moment, voice in the gulf, the nightmare articulated,
    the clock
naked, its back off, blood on the toiletpaper, the experience sung,
    done, Incanto,
the brain squeezed then released to drink back up what it bled—
Clarity & Vividness, both miracles, wed—At last—
    For a moment—
No more death.

S SONNET

No more child. Much less fathering
therefore. Much less mothering to know.
It (the child) eats what it loves. Cannibals
we are all cannibals. While mothering her
she herself starved. Then when the food was gone
she sat up, like Frankenstein's bride. Deformed,
dazzlingly haired & eyed.
A huge baby with a used heart.
So as for fathering and mothering
ask no mother, no father, what is that art.
What is that art? Tangles; tasks; tied.
As for me, I know much less therefore
for having done it. Without which ignorance
we die.

§ THE PHOTOGRAPHS

The photographs will never go crazy.
They are free, the slaves.
Since we can still change we can still go crazy.
That's why we keep returning to the photographs.
They seem so sane. They aren't. Without you
Crazy thing
They're nobody.

§ TRYING TO FEEL IT

The voice is in the dirt.
It wasn't for what she did
It was for what she suffered.
Which is not my hurt.
So I write this. So I
Try to give birth. Me,
A man.

§ IN DEBT

There are things you can't pay back
anybody. Not drunk,
not stoned on kindness,
nothing. Not lying is an art so few accomplish
no one should relinquish it. You can die
or you can stop it.
Clearest. Prettiest. Deadest.
You can't pay it back it's a zero its lips are shut.
The semen has crystallized enroute.
The menses is backed up in the pillow.
Not drunk, not stoned on kindness can it be undone
or forgiven. If it asks more
mail them the nightmares.
Shoot them with guns that squirt blood.
Pay them back.

§ DÉJÀ VU AGAIN

Love went riding in a hearse
With me behind her in the flower car.
We stopped beside a hole where she
Was put by men who could not see.
I did not know we had just come there to rehearse.
It burns before me like a tree
Aflame with treeness, clear and whole.
I wish my thoughts could see their fill
Of that invisibility.
They never will. I see and see and see the film
Of the cadillac in which Love rode
With me behind her in the flower car,
Dressed fit to kill.

I write of nothing.
Nothing's pure.
It slaves my brain.
Its chains are waves.
Its lock's a lure.

Humans come and go like hairs.
Leukemia flies through the air.
I write with my eyes.
Her thighs are tight.
My cock's no cure.

Some night we will disappear:
A shock of glare, a flight of ears.
A wave will lure us out of here.
I write of nothing.
Nothing's clear.

Golden are the bones of woe.
Their brilliance has no place to go.
It plunges inward,
Spikes through snow.

Of weeping fathers whom we drink
And mother's milk and final stink
We can dream but cannot think.
Golden bones encrust the brink.

Golden silver copper silk.
Woe is water shocked by milk.
Heart attack, assassin, cancer.
Who would think these bones such dancers.

Golden are the bones of woe.
Skeleton holds skeleton.
Words of ghosts are not to know.
Ignorance is what we learn.

Can't eat death
Like teacake shadow,
Can't eat that.
Chomp chomp of russian novel
Can't eat russian novel snow-on-horseflesh
Nor vodka eyeballs of madman eat
No no.
Can't eat brain itself & can't eat
Thoughts of mom-milk, gone, all gone,
Hush now.
Yet the banquet goes on.
Yet the banquet goes on.
Can't eat sleep.
Sleep eats me.
Day it eats
What Time can't be.
Dread is what we can't eat most. It tastes like ****,
It won't stay down.

§ MOMMIE SWIMS

Out of the toilet she comes, radiantly
empty. Drunk she looks like sylph
all enwound & gouged in the doorwhite, face
a mass embroidered like the flayed sciencebook man
enmuscled with live curled hair. She sways
and puts her hand against the wall
to steady the wall. Then approaches me
over the sliding rug, oriental, flying & enwrought
with absurd calm flowers turned from us
to drink themselves only. The bitches.
Who's that? A glass breaks, the bells fall
from the chimney the cymbals crash into the stick she
falls into the tub. A swimmer, she's a swimmer.
She sinks to seabottom in a little ball.
What a luxury flesh is. She vomits and is made whole.

A candle burns. The moon
is a skeletonhead again.
All day reassembling the car's engine
now 4 a.m. I lie down
and look at Anne for the first time
Mrs. Snowmelting and all the white wine drunk
save this one waterglass
I think will only breathe awhile
then also go mature among the words
like Anne the Wildman does
beside me breathing now one shoulder coral
one invisible and round under the sheet.
It's too late. Flux
comes to the bedroom door
and coughs. What skeletonheaded
thoughts she married
when I held her at Pontchartrain and she said
No No
in Catholic. A candle burns
for the dead female mutant human
whom we borrowed. The car still doesn't run.
But when I come to bed at 4
and she's been sleeping for five hours
Christ
how hot death's adolescence is.

Doved-out, drawn near, slowmotion
like castle collapse, sugar in the dark,
slim as a cut, a war movie, all the scores,
dealt the low burn, the bitch, the socko,
plucked, cashed in, the last kitten,
talked clear of the ink gleam where the train turns,
bent by dread, fenced, belled, self spilled, milk afire,
aquarium-eyed, no parking place, wallet lost,
beasteyes in the bush, fart in the elevator,
crayola broke, menstrual leak on white shorts
with blind date, thrown out bodily, screech-of-brakes wait,
the roast too raw, husband gone hearing leafcrunch,
throwing a rod, breaking a stud in the head, waiting
for the novocaine to work, drillstink, locking yrself out,
coplight in rearview mirror while drunk,
pretending to know an answer, caught
with your pants up, telling a lie on the phone,
stepping in it, shadow & act,
singing for your supper,
singing regardless.

§ SOME LAMB

That lamb
In skin
The black wink closes
On that *mnaah*
So dead
The film, the flesh
I guess
Is somewhere
Ecstasy
Is somewhere
Wed with sleep
In the bed
Armless headless pillow
Hold me
My pet lamb is leaping
Up! up! innocence is meat
Is what we live to eat
Straight up in bed
Twelve months
The night is fed
With shapes which fit so tight
This vest of ribs
We scream we beg
Time stop it! stop it!
And yet
That was
Some lamb
Some lamb
Says Death.

SOME LAMB

II. *After*

§ FOUR WOLVES

I tell this blackguy
who sits down at the table next to me in Kips
      hey man you dropped your matches,
he just nods, big felt hatbrim over all but his beard and his nod,
and he sees my half-full pitcher of beer and he says
      hey man can I have a shot of your beer?
and I nod yes and start to give him a drink from my glass
when this dude gets up and says,
      I'll get my own glass,
sits down, pours it full and then takes one of my cigarettes
and says to me I'm busted, disgusted, and not to be trusted,
and I say Well, I don't know about the first two,
and he laughs and claps his hands softly like
pleased at the innuendo of my comeback and then
the waitress comes up to his two sort-of buddies and tells them
they can't just sit there without ordering something, so one of them
   says
      hey man, can we sit with you, meanwhile
I've said nothing because look at what telling the dude
he dropped his matches
got me, so these other two dudes slide over to my table
and the one called Larry starts talking, mostly jiveass
lies, one after another stories about pussy and fights
in Chicago and a *whole* lot of stories about money and I just sit there
staring off real stone-like for awhile then
I pick up the pitcher and get it refilled
and two more glasses, which generosity you dig
these guys don't even acknowledge,
      so they all pour themselves beer and Larry says
Now Steve here he's been with some ugly women,
if you want a authority on ugliness Steve here
went into the ugly forest and the trees fell on his
      HEAD,
and Larry says, Man Steve he know women hurt people's feelins
just *lookin* at em,
and he tells about how he got stabbed three times and
six doctors was workin over him and when that dude stabbed me
I didn't hardly feel it, it was like somebody barely tappin you,
just like this, I mean bein stabbed don't hurt man it don't hurt and
I thought shit man, how come this dude ain't resistin don't he know

we are in a *fight,*
and Steve says hmmph occasionally,
and this goes on about twenty minutes during which
time they've hardly even touched their beers, which seems weird to
    me,
so I get up and go to the john and when I come back
they notice me, all three at once, and Larry says
Say man what's your name, and I tell him and he shakes hands
and Steve says his name is "Steve" and I see his eyes for the first time
under his big turned-down mean hatbrim and the other guy says
his name's Jo-Mo and I shake his hand
Berkeley style
and their eyes fall on me sincerely, which I interpret to mean
that they dig I haven't laughed artificially at their jive
unless the story really had wit to it, and they know
most white cats fake it 90 percent of the time
when around black guys and they don't even have
no *talent* to *their* lies, and all of a sudden
we were just shimmering there at the table
and nothing mattered & they were using language
& we were two floors up in this neon place waitresses
in black miniskirts and white aprons and the TV on
over the bar and the Budweiser ad horses rotating in the plastic
racetrack & the guy wiping out the big pizza oven
with a broom on a pole & other people at squares
of wood lit from above tables and pitchers of beer
dots of foam hurrying up & He's So Vain
playing on the jukebox & Dueling Banjos
& the bartender chewing a toothpick & there we were
outside all butchery
of TIME or CONTENT or RELEVANCE or NECESSITY
like four guys talking and shimmering on a stage in a play
written by the wolfman
in us all.

This is the sleep
Sleeping Beauty slept.
Dear Beauty, who didn't invite the Witch.
Dear Witch. O
it was cold.
O it was without Prince.
Thornbush swarmed in thornbush.
The years passed like years.
This is the sleep Snow White
lay down and slept the night
the Dwarfs wept. O
it was without Death.
And this is the sleep you've slept all week.
Poisoned needle, poisoned apple. Dear Anne
who met the Witch half way
met too much Witch. O it is later
forever.

§ SINGING DEATH

Illustrious one, in whom death is the vagrom wound
& who wanders on the wet grasses singing, sing no more
to me. I have heard your voice plenty & I hunger for health.
Yes, though it is beautiful & seduces, Hush. Come no more
glaze-eyed to my arms asking for pity then push me aside
when the urge strikes to start singing. Transfixed
& then unhinged, crazed with the wish to die & then with the fear
the wish might be granted. I have heard your song
and it shall not drag me yet down with it on the wet grasses.

Illustrious one, in whom death goes on living season by season,
drawing its strength from your singing, lovely
& deadly, Listen: I will not make myself
dead to nourish the death
blooming within you, vagrom intensity. Rather than that I'd see
you wandering lost on the white watery lawns at midnight
singing for the police to come get you, yes, even rather
see you staring at a white wall trying to sing the shapes
out of the whiteness than continue this dying together.

Illustrious one, in whom death is no longer a solid block
but a network, sing no more to me of the waterglass & the stopped
    clock.
Against such songs we've crashed enough, enough.
That which was from the heart and was heart's song
has been transformed, a heartless net in which to sing
is to struggle and suffer humiliation at the hour of death.
You who sing out of the vagrom flower-mouth-wound, go back!
The white grasses will release you, bones & voice & dress
one entity, dignity regained, deathsong left where you leave
your shape on the lawn in the wet blades. Singing yet.

Writing while listening
to Anne make the soft artificial thunder
of turning the pages of Newspaper.
And in the glass wall behind her
the reflection of me writing, listening
to what I write as I write down
what I hear as I watch us.

Many the dogs who chew
the loud bones on rugs
with heads turned sideways.
But how many men write poems
to make the picture and the version of the picture
one animal? How many dogs turn,
reflected, howling & changed,

to the fused fact and its flat version,
an ever-whitening bone
in mental passion? All her life
Anne makes the flash live in the picture
and all mine I sit typing,
turning my head sideways
the better to eat her.

§ BREAKING THE SILENCE

I look up drunk
at the female yard full of shadows.
Thunder no more, sky,
big sandwich gold & coral.
Suddenly I'm among them: the ordinary people.
Life is so difficult to train to talk.
So we get in the car and we drive, drive & drive,
and the white darkness around the gas station . . .
no no no! It's as if, changed by gasoline
into wiggling colors
the bits of sky stick to the windshield
and the aerial whips the trunk.
I'm among them also when they put their hands on their
outjutted hips and drink Cokes.
The dynamo art of simply kissing
roundmouthed by the Lake. Deep, deep,
you go crazy piecemeal
Mamma, you feel sinking, the screaming zipper,
and it's a slick place, a weasel, a swimmer,
that sex.
And I'm among them because they're everywhere
counting strokes of the gong & standing very still in the alley.
Well then? . . . ah, I have broken the silence
into mental whitemeat
of words. To what avail?
To tell the tale, to tell the tale.

Contrive a poem out of ears.
Tell it
so that its petals unchocolate
like a brain in a jar.
Wax walnut, melting with thought.
Make it a poem almost
lewdly knowledgeable
and make its knowledge
ooze, syrup from the punched trunk.
Make it snake up to the molecule whorey
and put its mouth
atomic against the mouth of its core.
Pull on its stem
to expose its foetus. Make it
have children with sleek ginger jaws,
make the dogs moan when it passes,
let it out of its jar,
make it lie with our corpse, our chaos.
Make it hungry, evil, enemy of Death.
Put it on paper. Read it. Make surgery
its sigh, and of such sting
the scorpions call it Jehovah & Who.
Make it now before you crap out.
Contrive it, sperm it, stroke it,
make it efficient, make it fit,
make it more poem than Poem can survive.

§ ANNE'S CURLS

I.

It's Sunday & the sun shines
through haze and gnats.
Daisy is sleeping horse-sleek
on the green rug
and Jazz Samba is playing.
The Catholics are flickering in the fence.
Our date last night
is still in me & I'm writing
out of that energy. It was good
to drink beer with you
and it was good to stop the fight
when no one else would & hand him his purple hat
& see the silver knife
slide on the black linoleum.
Because you were amazed and shiny.
It's still real.
If even Death can't kill it
then maybe it can't be killed. It's hard
to keep on loving someone
whose every mannerism reminds you
of a thousand failures. Mine
multiplied by yours until
we even resent each other's pleasures. How
can I make it right
what I ruined? Backwards
I can't see well. The footprints
instantly fill with water,
just little oval shines,
self-swallowing. Maybe
if I'd sought out a better doctor in Houston
Mouse would've lived longer.
Like you wanted to. Every
death's a murder. A million maybes.
I felt something rush back and forth
through our hands. I've always contended
an *angel* is anything seen with rapt attention, awe
making it shine & wave its wings.
I was amazed again, last night. Amazing.

2.

Last night at the bar with you
I saw you. A chocolate flower
melting there, like the egyptians
used to wear perfumed wax in their hair
that would melt during the party.
Shining stuff, an entire darkness done in
with every eyelash. Those eyes, inside them
my blue shirt reflecting, the candle
making your egypt cheekbones even deeper.
I could tell the difference between your
skin and your suede coat because your suede coat was cooler.
But behind the knee, no. It was one
immensity to grasp a single dot on the clock
that pleasure, like an eclipse of the sun
or infancy. I couldn't. It all goes so fast, Anne.
And part of it is all the superficials
gaining on sense until you *see* the thing.
A knife lying on a drum: like that.
Until the blade melts and we just
run together like two colors of water.

3.

Strange that I should need
your blackbrown curls
shining like water on chocolate
to make me see you again
as I saw you in Richardson.
Fear, fear is what makes
the trust between two people
feed on all the rotten things
we do. I thought the hair was blacker
in those other pants.
It was just flesh, unanimated
by what the brain brings
to the plunging in. Strange
that I should need a superficial

shape, an image of chaos
cunningly relaxed from flicker to flicker
to make my fear go away.
Underneath that mass of hair
the same brain plunges back and forth
I know. But I guess in all of us
illusion is active, the jazz
of browngold curls can erupt
in the head, the eyes can
see again the naked facts.
Maybe I shouldn't feel so guilty
that when your hair was straight
I didn't so much want to bury
my face in it. We crave change,
we fear sameness without it.

4.

Then the blackmanfight, two on one, I move to help . . .
linoleum-colored form
with twisted tentacle . . . I hand one his hat, purple,
bleeding nosebridge, the red blood looking thicker
against his dark skin . . . You won (I assure him, soothe him)
You won because you were innocent.
Standing there in the backrush of the timid . . . sad
because the whites thought "dogfight" . . . fled . . . let the dogs
gnash . . . Then sitting at the table again, my heart beating,
seeing the silver knife kicked under the black table.

5.

Dying of fear can't be confessed
to someone you fear. Last night
I didn't fear you, like I didn't fear you
five years ago. Was it because
your hair was curlier, your body slimmer,
your fingernails wet-looking?
Illusion & Substance

congeal with Actual Thing
to make a whole in the brain
that perceives it. By sex
we struggle between the two.
On the street outside the post office
& before in the alley between Penney's
and the parking lot we
struggle with it. "Would you like to walk with me
from *here to there?*" I ask insultingly.
I come back & find you are sitting on the steps,
really alone. You refuse my arm.
Two hours later we are really married.
To die of fear of revealing yourself
to the person who loves you is murder.

§ EXCELLENCE OF EXCESS

I.

Excellence of excess, ah yes.
Excellence of excess before we got scared.
Sexual labyrinth infinite no stopping.
Excellence of no stopping.
Being the Undead.
I dropped my friend's sunglasses into the sewer,
two ovals of cloud and glare.
Excellence of that unpremeditated evil. Ah,
buying him others to match. Excessive smoke
and dentyne mixed, mild aphrodisiac. Excellence
of the Undead in their cricket clothes, all
gloss and rub till numb of nipple lip and act.
The rouge pathway under the zebra awning beside the Granada.
Excess as tho excess were limit.
And silk slid down in the van and in the lightsoff pasture
& moisture gathering of badminton cloth in crack.
And we stayed excessively undead until we'd wrought our wrath.

2.

Now we've become the half dead. Partied
at the New Orleans House & lost our black pens of India &
danced with the dance. In the women's toilet went
to read the graffiti and found it abstract spiritual
and bland. Came out with hands behind
as reins for teetering Anne, the loved one again.
Past the giant mirror that looked at the dancefloor
like one of them was a hole in water. Past
the icecube room. Past the tables of others
furtively no-glancing up & down like guilt shy lambs.
Back to the floor stood leaning you soft and straight stock still I
mambo crambo to the organ, lax & jerking, your man,
scary electricity of other-person Anne in my hands.
Kissed with our Mouths.
Went to excess that we might be among the Undead again.

Tragic rabbit, a painting.
The caked ears green like rolled corn.
The black forehead pointing at the stars.
A painting on my wall, alone

as rabbits are
and aren't. Fat red cheek,
all Art, trembling nose,
a habit hard to break as not.

You too can be a tragic rabbit; green and red
your back, blue your manly little chest.
But if you're ever goaded into being one
beware the True Flesh, it

will knock you off your tragic horse
and break your tragic colors like a ghost
breaks marble; your wounds will heal
so quickly water

will be jealous.
Rabbits on white paper painted
outgrow all charms against their breeding wild;
and their rolled corn ears become horns.

So watch out if the tragic life feels fine—
caught in that rabbit trap
all colors look like sunlight's swords,
and scissors like The Living Lord.

§ DOG

Dog you are an idiot.
Standing beside my chair
rainy day
eyes goofy gold, ever-hungering.
Impossible to feed you enough.
Impossible to fill your brown bowl.
I think we are similar.
As the angel beats in the drape
so do we stare at one another.
Man at dog, dog at man, over the gulf.
Yet sometimes you make me happy.
When I put on my jacket and you *know*
and you leap like a small horse.
What does riding in the car mean to you, I wonder.
No answer. Always the same brainless
bolt through the door, knocking people over,
up through the car window like a cat
through a hoop of fire.
Dog you complicate my life.
I can't move with you.
I can't bear the guilt of getting rid of you.
I sometimes think you are as intelligent
as a creature should get. Not really.
I'm glad I'm human. I'm glad I'm not a dog.
OK, Daisy, time to eat.
I know you don't like to go out in the rain.
I'll feed you in the kitchen.
BUT DON'T GET ANY SLOP ON THE FLOOR.
And she nods.

I.

Out comes that shining length
all scales & eyeslits
from the mud.
That was 31 years ago. Ink
snake swallows ink sun
if you paint it that way.
Meanwhile, cheekcheek, cheekcheek
go the sparrows in the spanish roof
up the street. Where the curly
silver terrier barks behind the window.
These are songs, these are meant to be spoken.
Oh, now the snake is broken.
Glass juts sideways from a lamb
if you kill it with kisses.
But if you just write down the words
the rest will be birthings.

2.

Couth as silk, what shaking and warming of worms
ends as this embroidered skirt? A miracle
lays its bleeding head
on the tapestry. How do you make them breed?
You shake and warm them on a screen
then pull their tentacles until they purr
then slice their undersides with tissue.
Impossible to measure the droplets
that cling to the wiper. Thus
comes the splurge of flowerlets
that is reputed to sweeten the mind.
But this is yet to be proved.
The screen must not touch the ground.
Also, beware of cats. You won't know
the cats are eating them because silkworms have no voice.

3.

Many times I have not heard them, the
grunting & screaming slugs
heading for my dog's waterbowl.
Singer, put a nickel
next to that silk flower Sally
has made lay on her thigh. Then
sing it to sleep so that we can get on
with the flashlight & hammer slaughter of the slugs.
Is this an ornamental tangle
of Images? I guess. Yet so is Sally,
undressed, silk rose pulsing in her pants.
So which of them is less realistic?

4.

Irrational monologues
placed beside the more familiar Tongues
constitute the one mouth
that slaves in the wall we have built
to protect us from eavesdroppers.
So it goes. Things sing.
Maniacs (the imaginations of ants) mumble for mamma.
Then through the hairnet of branches
the sun melts together the veins of the sentences.
He is reputed to have fed his violin
to the sausage machine. But that's crazy.
More likely it was a monologue
that went askew. He went walking
and was run down by a motorist
in whom death was wrestling. It only
looked like his violin lay
in the sunlight in its transparent condom.

5.

Finally we come round to the art of common speech,
as though in a canoe smoothly
past the black strawberries.
Yes, the man says, but surface is holy. Ah,
plain speech, plain, as under the rock bridge
the rock bridge reflects.
And the sun bobs in the flycast pool.
And in the fishingbarge bags of blood
hang down, bait for the bass. What's so
plain about that? And if in a song I should write
"past the black strawberries"
why should one look for reference
as a hook? The canoe heals what it wounds.
Behind us, the common poem.
Glass going: wah wah wah wah wah.

6.

Goodnight, mouthflower. Gloxinia
with the snowhite hole and the purple trumpet.
By the brass bells. By the chess set,
castles and horses
turned. By love & fear the sentences join
their absurdities. Long & sleek, hungry, plush,
cuntcock, inordinate, gash in chalk,
vocal, by love unhung. What does the lack
imply? One-eyed gloxinia, good night
to the pistons & the rice. The motif turns.
The artificial frog crawls the fountain wall.
The mouths proliferate in the same world
that their songs call into life.

It would have done no good,
judged dead & shadow of fire in the icehouse,
to have spoken up against the snakes in the bloodstream
that swallowed her eggs
& herself. It would have done
no good.
Screaming in the scream-multiplying hospital linoleum corridors
O O O O O
would have altered not one eye turning
bright & oily to her window where she sighed
"Goodnight, moon" at the moon between bars of the bed.
It would have lifted no hairs up
like light in a quartz to have ordered Death
back where he came from, back to the car.
It would have done no good to have whispered
in any of her ears that this was It, that now
she is part of the vast drift that even
the molecules in the bedpan enact.
Nor had we sung together
ah ah ah ah ah
in the fatherly icehouse flamethrower last instant
when the heart went Nope
would it have been different than it was:
Hideous & Good.

Broken flowers, tender thing
strewn,   , pitchfork & woodwork mute,
          , fishflash deceived and a hook
          , buried in the pretty
feather,   , dilation of the mainspring, pressure
on a man, a woman, to be cleansed by plunging,
          , the highest altitude at which milk will boil
calculated, in snowshoes, his heart a rock,   , broken,
tender thing no more, a quart measure
of redstuff,   , blank places in the logic,
      self-pitying muteness,
tear me a sheet of paper
from the tablet called Mean Sheen, right now, before it tears
itself,   , half of Friday being a pig by its heels,   , the
          other half
eat,   , air was that child now air again
whom the substance searches,   , strawman hugs torch, perch
swallows pretty hook, a man or a woman,
          , the least of them,
despair that the tenderness can't be put back together,
acetylene's only friend,   , and even it molten, and even it
broken.

§ EXCESS IS EASE

Bend down, bend down. Excess
is the only ease,
so bend. The sun is in the tree.
Put your mouth on mine. Bend down
beam & slash, for Dread is dreamed-up-scenes
of what comes after death. Is being
fled from what bends down in pain.
The elbow bends in the brain, lifts the cup.
The worst is yet to dream you up,
so bend down the intrigue
you dreamed. Flee the hayneedle in the brain's tree.
Excess allures by leaps. Stars burn clean. Oriole
bitches and gleams. Dread is the fear of being less
forever. So bend. Bend down and kiss
what you *see*.

§ THE DAZZLES

1.

A great dazzle: & then
it is as tho the sea has fed enough.
The shadow of the tree
rises on the coral wall
of the apartmenthouse across the street: & then
is engulfed, is a meal.

2.

Daisy puts her animal paw on my arm: & then
the dazzle drains, vanishes,
is swallowed. Even the silence of the hedge
is Illusion. So drunk these days
I can't distinguish what I have dreamed
from what really happened: & then
even the paradox dazzles.
And what is not "food"?
What?

3.

Eating. Walking in my garden being eaten.
Pondering in the mottled light on the bookpage: & then
a dazzle enters the mind, a fusion of dazzles.
I look up. The shadows are logical.
The logic is perfect & butchered.

§ SNAKEMARRIAGE

In disquiet to my bed
You hungeringly come.
The craft of it amazes,
The art of it can not be undone.
Words dumb, for they were always so
And the luggage yawns.
So we both be travellers
Toward the hungry & disquieting center
Slowly, slowly, like the skin of snake
Unsheathes the new wet monster in it.
Word-eaters both, groom & bride,
The craft of it is excess, the art won't wait.
I saw you glimmer so
I thought an icicle had grown hair & sides.
The hole slid back its hood and spoke,
And what it said no craft or art can show
In common language. Now in disquiet
We slowly, slowly thrive
On what our luggage closed upon and ate.
The craft of sincerity and the art of hate
Mingle to make a single snake,
More length than depth, more hiss
Than fang, more like craft & art
Than human speech dare call mere *love*
Or whatnot.

§ ADVOCATING MELANCHOLY

I stand by the drainboard advocating
the wisdom of melancholy.
The young man who uses words as a pedant uses them
uses them. I turn back to the pale yellow wine in my cup.
And try to explain:
we hang between two seemingly irreconcilable facts,
the capacity to Sing & the inevitability of Death.
The whales, the birds at daybreak,
sing out of melancholy.
The young man keeps asking questions
that indicate my words
are only words to him.
So I turn my attention to the pale yellow wine
and the remembered name "Ginger Mang"
of her cat.

§ LOOK!

Look! she is dead: no cover can cover her: look,
her hands are dead just as her face is dead: all of her is dead:
where is the soul? she looked no lighter on the pillow when it went.
My eyes fill with water that falls from under my sunglasses:
when the bells ring: even the oxygen grieves:
surely this is not what she was meant for:
look! a shaft of light pierces the dustball: just that effortlessly

she went.

Hide me
from me.
Fill these
holes with eyes
for mine are not
mine. Hide
me head & need
for I am no good
so dead in life
so much time.
Be wing, and
shade my me
from my desire
to be
hooked fish.
That worm
wine
looks sweet and
makes my me
blind. And, too,
my heart hide
for I shall at
this rate it also
eat in time.

§ FOUR DAYS IN ANOTHER CITY

I.

At Jack's.
This is Los Angeles.
This is where Mouse said,
                    When a thing gets rusty
            it looks more like a sculpture.—
Jack & Carla (tall friends both) lie
arm over covers, embraced
in the tiny room—Anne is on the foldout couch
and the birds are chortling—but sitting Where?—
    No trees on this neat little American
    first-baby street—I'm told
    Los Angeles
    is all around me
    even as I write this
    growing—Well, there's the bowl before me on this
maple table before the fern & fuchsia kitchen
seven huge lemons 2 apples
                    the shadow of my moving pen,
                    the forked one—
                            is that not proof
enough?—Even
            the language remembered
            is sculpture—
it never stops, it never just exhales
its drunk-as-mud-memory
and goes lie down among the ivy, exhausted,
no more to peep thru sight toward insight,
no more the rainbow's one curve
be plunged both ends in others' mouths—
    this is the city talk turned its back on,
    this is the city
    of the Angels.

2.

Leaves have blown up at the gate.
The oily oxblood top leaves of the hedge

are sticking straight up.
The dirt is packed grassless.
I sit at a foreign table,
noting. The toilet warbles. The clouds
go their ways. The TV aerial is spreading
its skeleton wings. The timegulch
closes its lips again. Sleepy voice in other room,
jingle of spare change as a man puts on his pants,
thump of bare foot hitting the floor,
stir this blue room,
wake and be witnessed
Sir Miracle, Miss Angel-of-Moves.

3.

Pouring blaze, snowflake-fern, voiceless
& cherry-of-the-mind, no History
nor tangle of grass
can imitate the brain's receiving, Jack's
a father now, Jack's shadow is larger than ever.

4.

At Mike's.
Birds come from out of the parched mountain
to sit in his olive trees.
   There is this great thing,
   this lengthy beast
     they come out of—even its name shakes
   as we watch it imitate change—moths
   that noiselessly beat
   in the ivy, gnats-too-small,
   the leaves clapping,
   the bird's raw cry in the bush
   that rises in tone like a question
asked the millionth millionth—
not to be "answered,"
but to Tell—to let this great thing know

this beak, *these* lips—forget the others
or remember them—
        but *these*
you must once more listen
ask it—
   and the mountain slopes upward
   into the scalding silence—down from which
the wholeness, the allness, the answer
         Beasts & Calms.

5.

Tempting to place in coherent collage
     the bee, the mountain range, the shadow
     of my hoof—
tempting to join them, enlaced by logical
     vast & shining molecular thought-thread
     thru all Substance—
and yet I only guess it,
or intuit it,
or wish it—
     the bees here have black bottoms with white bands
     and they sit for a long time on weedblades
     as tho thinking
     and nowhere in any direction a flower and
     a single spiderstrand turns & twinkles
     porch to olivetree 50 feet and behind me
     the murmur of Anne & Mike
     behind patio glass—Tempting
to say I see in all I see
the place where the needle
began in the tapestry—but ah,
it all looks whole *and* part—
long live the eyeball and the lucid heart.

6.

4pm.
The mountains are in haze.
Wood dove is cooing in the grove.
The potted plant is creaking on its chain.
The leaves blow and then the leaves calm.
Not death haze, just enough to make
the folds and the bulges
blend. The silence outlogics the heat.
We will see what

we will see.

7.

Back at Jack's.
I'm back at the fern window
& blownleaf gate—the De Govia boy's face
   is a ball of light—
   the last such
   torch on its neckstalk
   that wore clothes and walked
   got plunged in blood
   and stopped—
no matter—the lightbulb forgives the electricity—
the blame is ubiquitous,
it sheds equally,
it fathers and unfathers simultaneously,
It Arts.

8.

Now the mountain
is the remembered mountain
and the black pen
these solos
run from

also dwells in Time
potential flash
held back from Mind
to plunge in
perfect pool
now no more literal
than ever
lost in Thought's
round shine
a lamp on its stick
all changed by talk
into remembered roar
and witnessed
more or less
as all deeds done in Fact
go backwards
out of Substance
into Mental Hat
to await the magician
with the talking hands
to pull them back
just as this black pen
pulled one way by Things
and one by Thoughts
gives you this
kissed-by-language-rabbit
take it
a black one & a white one
for god's sake take it
before it dies
and becomes
Literal Thing again
mere madeless mute
and barren rabbit,
only ink.

How keep dark
and pattern that any man suffers
off—at the wall, at where the hat
comes out of the marrow & yawns—
how keep head up the scream
& up the burial where the pattern is born—
how the leagues washing their hearts
& wrung dry only to sponge back up—men
smooching mirrors—blades honing—
tongue & eyelash of Sweet Thing
staggering the shape by the door in the baggy shadow—
how keep dark back?
Or should one bullet-forth, sleek-clothed or naked—pierce
each entity—each clock—sharpened by art
or wine—how
enter the needle, the cloth—
how take the pattern any man suffers
and lose nothing when you
rip it off.

BODY OF WORK

§ AMERICAN RAIN

The wet street looks like hammered tin.
The streetlights say 'O' in the mist.
Be sweet, be sweet! The meat lifts up its skirt of skin
and underneath is what we feared:
a candle with a silver beard.

The dead don't share.
Though they reach toward us
from the grave (I swear
they do)
they do
not hand their hearts to you.
They hand their heads,
the part that stares.
The dead do not look like
The Dead. The nightmare is
they live the life, wear shiny shoes,
and smile the smile, and comb
real hair. But what they give is not the gift.
They squeeze our hearts *as if* to eat.
They cannot have. They dare not want. This
is their Art.

Wrecked on the wine, on wreckage
itself. Wrecked on what
some call
the dog.
Wrecked when the heater goes on,
when the horn honks.
Waking and sleeping
all in a row. Not drinking the turkey.
Drinking the turkey.
Wreckage of remembering, wrecked
voice on telephone.
Burying the never-to-be-forgotten bone.
Ten ton flakes of light
falling from skyscraper.
Shrugging them off.
Face wrecked by thoughts.
The wine rolling its tongue. Teeth
wrecked by dog
of dread. Of what then. Of course.
What the wreck loves
to absorb, turn red with.
Buried under the thing buried above.
Guest rat chewing the wall.
Wrecked on facts, the shark,
the changeless photograph,
dog's balls.
Celebrating wreckage raw.
3 a.m. nightmare wine
poured on the wound. It yawns.
Her coat her ghost she's gone.
Losing the haystack finding the needle,
Singing along with the wrecking ball.

You enter the movie
you enter. You and your fears
trade places. Horses
eat black grass in white daylight.
Everyone is at the instant of ecstasy.
Everyone has the bullethole eyes of prophets.
Agony becomes solvable.
It isn't a dream; it isn't a dream.
Doors open on rooms
where irrationally gleaming giant faces
have laid their thoughts on tables
like so many sausages.
The invisible has started to look like a penis.
It isn't despair to see it.
The strangeness is a solace. It seems right
that the black grass the white horse is eating
emits music. When its mouth moves
our eyes move.
You could see a skeleton
hand in a suede glove
if you saw it. Irrelevancies
in the lives of nobodies
change you. It isn't evasion of clarity.
Both. Both. Feelings
shake and crow in the halfgloom
stars of the plaster ceiling.
A girl appears in a dress of solid dress-shaped light.
A horse appears naked.
So that we exceed what we fear
for a flash of time that isn't Time
in the literal. Irrational Light Talks.
An old man has a heart attack
in the tomatoes. You believe it. You must
or you'll be doomed to live it.
Death is allowed but deadness isn't.
The light-wedge widens as it reaches
the place where the faces are needed.
Because we need to die very often.
So that we'll never be dead while *in* it.

§ POEM ON CRAWLING INTO BED: BITTERNESS

The dogs and angels stalk each other.
Their tongues are planks.
How dramatic.
Barking or sighing, the song's the same.
The floor is rotten
in the Paradise Lounge. Below
is the attic.
Being no swimmer,
I step out and breathe.
Ink has been poured down the flatness
where sky meets matter. All's well.
I've outlived Jesus.
Some things lighten nightfall
and make a Rembrandt of a grief.
But mostly the swiftness of time
is a joke; on us. The flame-moth
is unable to laugh. What luck.
The myths are dead. Over the horizon
the purring bloodless angels
of disembodied intelligence
sizzle and blink.
I have kissed a cannibal.
Wings stir the sunlit dust
of the cathedral in which
the Past is buried
to its chin in marble.
Dogs and angels differ
and lying with a naked woman
is better than the butchery of relativism,
and the paradise of beer and lobster
vanishes in the body; which has its own logic.
Dogs howl. Angels primp. The brain's an error.
The comic is the last perspective,
and Nature is a stupid teacher,
and the dogs and angels are considering marriage.

The melancholy elephant
is eating lettuce
in the light from the hole
in the concrete roof
of her heaven.
I am laughing, laughing!
For I have never seen
such a spectacle
as the way she closes her eyes
when she chews, or
tilts her head sideways
as she stuffs the lettuce
deep down her throat.
The sliding of dryness
into moisture nearly makes me
break down, on my knees,
in the laugh-echoing
elephant house. This beast
should not, can not, be
my sister, nor I
her smooth brother, in any sense
fruit from the same tree.
Yet I have seen the maps
of growth in the books.
They say that not only
is the elephant I, but that I
am you. It nearly
makes my ribs un-spring
to think amoeba could do, did do,
both things. So I should be happy,
happy, when it's midnight
and the elephants are doing
what the elephants do at midnight,
and I am melancholy too,
that we are food in the same jaws,
under the same brain,
that revolve and drool in the Void.

Smoke beshags
the lemons and olives.
I was not mad.
I have color slides to prove this.
If you see a flayed goat
hanging in a Haitian shack
tell that goat I have a color slide
this side of death; its death.
And that the veins are still violet.
Further: I have evidence
all history is the orange
of blood-stained water.
Here come the lemons from their gallows.
Silk dress, head of spinach, chicken on her bones.
I have this documented.
History: madness: how did they stuff that man's bones
into that jar whose mouth is smaller than his head?
The chalk gasps. And the fish filet
bears the pink imprint of the bones
of the fish that was in it.
You will make a beautiful fossil
because you believe in ideas.
The tapestry was reversed
so that we could see what madness
resembles. If you see that goat tell it
I have a color slide of the metaphor
of its death. I did not suffer madness.
I suffered facts.
And have the bloody photographs to prove it.

There's no fleeing the cry-bird. This evening
a dove walked on the air mattress in my pool
on squashy careful claws.
I'm on a journey fleeing the cry-bird.
Last Sunday, at the ballpark, guess what they gave me:
a razor! Later, in the warehouse of antiques
where I went to flee her
there were the beast-horned armoires and crazed mirrors
lined up as though stunned by their own distinctness.
Is that the refuge? that luminous dumbness
utterly lost in Thingness? How can a human
flee into objects? The cry-bird was perched at every aisle.
Her whistling plus the thump of the heart in the wall
drove me back onto the street. So I took my sunglasses
out of my shirt and now am here.
This strange thing happened, he said. A bird
flew into my apartment and now it's in the bathroom.
And there, on a shelf, in a fern,
was a myna bird. He swore it had not said a word.
Well then, I said, it's not the cry-bird.
He stared as though waiting for the rest of the sentence.
I asked her what six months of catatonia was like.
Well, she said, it was mostly pretending. Most
insanity is pretending but you wait for somebody
to give you a good reason to stop it.
And she laughed like an intelligent little demon.
She said she wears all that make-up to hide the scars
on her face. And I said, What scars?
And she ran two fingers from her lip to her ear.
No! I refused to settle for anything less
than what is analogous to jumping in icewater. Up,
with characteristic squeaking, flapped the dove.
Which she humorously insisted rhymed with "stove."
Silly girl. Don't you realize
we are supposed to be fleeing the cry-bird?
She stared at me like a boy at his first adult
vagina. What a metamorphosis! Terrified,
and allured. You mean you really believe
I'm a person worth liking? she asked, almost in tears,
more than almost. Cree! Cree! the cry

of her double. What can't be fled must be re-invented.
The cry-bird does not roost in the apple tree
but there's a nest somewhere or it couldn't go on
and on. A razor, no less!
So we all fled on.

Tenderness toward women: to accomplish
the passing over
from fear into tenderness.
To begin again there. The Flesh Door
kicked in.
To learn not to hate the original tenderness
that rendered you helpless.
To not kill the mother again. Once
being enough. To consider your penis
neither noodle
nor .38 caliber.
To figure out what is going on
in a particular instant.
Tenderness is Paying Attention.
The price otherwise is estrangement.
Which even if you win
you do not accomplish.

§ WHAT HAPPENED WHEN THE MILK CAME OUT

The girls were burying the dead
robin
when he came up and saying
That's stupid
stabbed the trunk.
Everyone knew
when you stabbed that tree
milk came out.
Everyone knew it.
He knew it.
I thought
How come some seem
to like
death, I mean *like*
it? That's girl's
stuff he said wiping
the milk off on
his pants.

He said, "Let me look
at your breasts." As she undid the buttons
the blouse shook. She said,
"You too," and he did—and later
saw the event as a series of snapshots—
it was that intense. "You too,"
she said, and put
her ear
against his hard, flat chest; deafening;
and she felt the dissolving wholeness
of medieval angels, and the buckle jingled
as it slid.

I hear my neighbor's "cuckoo,"
my wife's slipper scraping from rug to toilet,
and turning I see the chameleon
come down to Drink and Peer.
It sings the hour, her cuckoo, and over the hall rug goes
its solo.
I place the newspaper on the couch,
I hear her breathing in the bedroom,
and she half mad awaiting my permissions, and I like that
neon chameleon its throat pulsing
its whole body
rigid.
Cuckoo, cuckoo, cuckoo: nine times
as I walk with the *Picayune*
up the corridor beside her door, through which
I heard one evening mournfully singing
& saw the door open once
& everything seemed made of bamboo.

A snapshot:
> *Shirtless blackman loading sacks of flour*
> *into a boxcar*
> *white powder on black sweatgleam*
> *like two people in the same pants.*

I stare down into the garden
as she turns the pages.
What analogies survive
the Real?
Clock coughs.
A knock at the gate . . . "Come in
oh sweet Southerner with hair parted on both sides,
bowing and making the moment lustrous. For I have been
a prisoner in both camps
and I can assure you. . . ." And lay listening

to the clock until the black leaves were fanged with blue.
And over & over in Dream
carried out the same idiot package,
the same ransom of snakes. "I can assure you. . . ." And

sat at the tombgate laughing & knocking.
Cuckoo. Cuckoo.

A snapshot:
>   *Red handkerchief-head black mama six foot*
>   *six cotton dummy outside pralineshop eee*
>   *ternal smile.*

"I'm tired of everything always being a battle,
I'm tired of always putting what you want first
as though what I wanted was by definition crazy or neurotic,
I'm *tired* of my needs being just plain less important
as though some god were measuring feelings on a scale
and could say that what you want measures ten pounds
and what I want measures three . . . !"

until

I am sitting in The Blue Monkey,
Vieux Carré, on a stool in The Blue Monkey Vieux Carré
beside a lady storage-battery
in bulging green, by the knit cleaved at the neck
and a scarlet earring revolving with the earth;
outside the monkey doors
is a luminous ditch between buildings
the tourists row with their legs;
I am extremely drunk;
I am at one of those zeniths
when all dangers and all safeties are equal;
then, just as suddenly as saying it,
I'm squatting in a vegetablestink doorway and bending over me
is the silver jaw of a drunk
who keeps calling me "brother,"
who thinks we are in the same boat, go away, go away, ah!
the tourists avoid my gaze, *I* have become the odious lump,
and who knows, knife under khaki? I have passed
into the ultimate disguise, invisible
even to myself; squatting gaze fixed on moving faceovals
that bloom and slam shut,
detached into a kind of serenity;

tranquilly passes the two-layered bayou of flesh, tranquilly
the cattle following the one before who follows
the one before who follows the one who thinks it hears
the bell.

It looks like rain
looks.

I can see her lips moving I know she is talking.
I have entered the mirror ventriloquists sit in.
The clacking mouths of their dummies slowly become pliant.
Everything is kissing itself.
But all I can hear is the self-sized, parrot-pure whisper,
"chickenshit, chickenshit, chickenshit."

It was about to rain,
so I was walking between two buildings
when I came upon a pile of baseball caps
which were obviously being thrown away,
so I knelt and began trying them on
when along passed two young women (one of them
very pretty), and we nodded, and I returned my attention to
        the caps
when the pretty one came back, and knelt beside me,
and then her hands were in my hair and her mouth
on mine wet and taking and yielding and while I was
        astonished
I was also willing to see where this went,
at which point it began to rain very hard
which I could see from the corner of my eye
was ruining the caps, and I thought Shit,
I really wanted one of those caps, and then I realized
to my further astonishment that although it was raining on us
we were not getting wet, at which point her partner
whom I had barely noticed, slipped her hand between my legs
from behind and I thought Now wait a minute now
this is actually getting a little scary I mean
what if one of them has a knife? but nothing happened
and who am I? so I put my hand along the pretty one's side
and began gently to fondle her breast, at least I

thought it was gentle, at which point she said Hey!
and pulled back like I was trying to Start Something,
and I felt this wave of embarrassment and injustice
because I was completely minding my own business
when she started this and now she acts like I'm
the rapist, so then all her actions take on this very
touch-me-not tone while at the same time
her partner has actually unzipped my pants and is
slowly working her fingers inside, well I can tell you
the contradictory information coming in at both ends
of my body was about more than I could handle and that's all
I can remember.

"chickenshit . . ."

A snapshot:
>I ask the alcoholic-faced gas station owner
>Where is the Lafayette Cemetery and he says
>Up Washington about five blocks in the niggers
>the tour busses don't stop there no more I'm
>telling you these niggers.

A wave of embarrassment and injustice
as I realize that we, the two white ones,
have climbed into the backseat, and he,
the black one, is driving and to anyone outside
it looks like two little white dolls
being chauffeured, at which point he spots
a pair of nurse's shoes in a trashcan
and stops the car and gets back in
and holds them up in his
black hand they are blinding.

The blue monkey, the blue monkey. ". . . all you do
is make up excuses to justify your own fears
and I'm tired of playing second fiddle to your refusal
to risk anything I'm thirty-three years old and for five years
I've been living in that same apartment just because
you didn't want the hassle of something like
having our mail forwarded well I'm

tired of giving in just because the cost of winning
is too great . . . !"
The blue monkey,
the blue monkey,
the gasjets beautiful in the darkness.

Perish the thought
and the senses perish.
And when the senses are flooded
as in a cathedral
thought perishes
and is reborn repeatedly.
And when the senses at carnival
yield to the deluge, the excess,
all the Identity you have carved in thought
perishes like a monkey
on a stove's crownshaped gasjets in darkness,
bluer & bluer as he vanishes.

And the rain is brain-colored.
And the thunder sounds like something remembering
        something.

I.

All morning the birds
answeringly whistle in the turning
fog-black pines. *All of us are darlings,*
they say. *All of us are among the called.*
We go numb like a squirrel on a log touched by cat
or at footsteps on gravel of an approaching god.
Lord, we implore, make the birds sing a rational song,
make us all giants among forms!
And a ladder came down from the sky—
and a burning form dismounted—
and it said, "I have brought you a message"—
and I said, "Get off my property"—
and it smiled and massaged its temples.
All morning the audible but invisible birds
whistle as though lost or confused, calling and being called
to the tulip tree by the bay window
at the far end of the livingroom
of Heaven.

2.

The man on television
said he died
and went to Heaven
and came back
the same doctor in the same eyeglasses.
"Look at me! I was transparent. Do you know why?
Because the last drop of blood had been shed
for me, by Him. For there are no organs in Heaven.
I was neuter. I had no voicebox. I picked a flower.
It was waterless. For He is the moisture in Heaven.
I had a beautiful body. Anyone would have known me.
Only not so beat up."
And he squeezed his hands between his knees
and stared at the rug
as though it were the rug
of Heaven.

3.

Who are these shades we wait for and believe
will come some evening in limousines
from Heaven?
The rose
though it knows
is throatless
and cannot say.
My mortal half laughs.
The code and the message are not the same.
And what is an angel
but a ghost in drag?

4.

Camelia, I pity you
the scorched hood with no eyeholes
you are forced to wear
in this, your first Heaven.
I look upon you as a fragment of spirit
dislodged so that I might
walk on these slippery bricks at midnight drunk
on wine and in a traditional melancholy,
with my sword and my tongue.
To cut your throat would be no more difficult
than saying the word . . . *slit* . . .
peel back the hood to the bruised skull beneath it.
Your camelia-brains shivering
and an iceman standing above them
with a flashlight and pail.

5.

The elevator lady at the Beverly Wilshire
who is aging now but once was surely delicate and pretty,
and who seems to have this meaningless job
running the automatic elevator in white gloves
as a charity so that she can be near the Stars,
and who seems to walk a fine line
between the Real and her own Delusions, tells me
they have people from all over the world
working in their hotel, and, pointing
to a black man polishing a mirror
just as the elevator doors close, says,
"Did you see that man? He's from Hades.
He was a lawyer there but he's working in the hotel
while he goes to school and learns English."

Babble of shadows.
The doors noiselessly meeting.
The effeminate and eternally exasperated deskclerks
cursing their powerful underlings.
"They had *no* authority to *tell* you that!"

The days are like the whitemeat of a crab.
They face the ocean.
If only I had acquired the skill of empathy.
What you take for granted will destroy you.

I leave the elevator and go into the bar.
There's a wooden rooster on the cash register.
In line to get boarding passes at the airport
was a Hell's Angel carrying a Samsonite attache case
behind a nun carrying a flyrod. I smile
at the juxtaposition. For lunch I drink the bar's
white plastic trash barrel of cold sweat.
Enough of cuteness!

I go out to the hotel pool.
There falls to my attention
a sleeping woman, chin
in palm, elbow
on the arm
of the lawnchair.
She was reading
when she began breathing
more heavily.

One of us is in Heaven.

6.

All around me, cooing in the fogpines, are the angels
who are always patient, who live on dew and commands.
I see them thrusting their little testicle-shaped heads
with the black necklaces encircling
the place where the skullcaps stop,
thrusting in the pinefog's swimming and smoky blackness,
the literal world.
I say, *"Break down my door oh small angel with rosebud mouth*
standing on gnarled branch speaking like water
running on silverware, break down my door!"
And it rustles.
And everything has two meanings.
And the petals of the tuliptree
at the far end of the livingroom
make the path slippery,
the path to Heaven.

§ METAPHYSICAL SHOCK WHILE WATCHING A TV CARTOON

Things come from nothing.
The lawnmower
the bulldog uses
to shave the cat
in the cartoon I am watching:
from nothing.
The startled duck bursts
from nothing; drags its feet in the water;
doubles the glaze.
Suddenly, where there was nothing,
there is a lawnmower.
In the next scene the cat is not shaved.
Its hair has returned spontaneously,
and the bulldog's jowls are overlapping
a big naked bone which then
is a stick of dynamite which explodes the dog's head.
In the next scene the dog's head is a dog's head again.
Nothing did it, and nothing
made it ok. The logic of the cartoon
overwhelms me. I watch the TV in the mirror
over the fireplace to get some perspective. But this just
doubles the nothing. *I* came
from where that lawnmower came from.
Jesus, I whisper. I'm frightened, and write down
on the telephone message pad the first line
of this poem; itself, especially, suddenly,
from nothing.

§ CYCLE

A severe Spring; shortening shadows
     fall on a snowcrust.
There is nothing and there is something;
twin dreads mate
     and my bed is empty
     but for cool me.
The treefrogs come back; the cicadas
     kick the crumbs from their tombs
     and crawl the treetrunks
     and die.
As far as eye sees, or mind imagines:
severity.
Where am I bound? Leisure
has eaten my slippers and the days do not end
they stop. The lemons are green: not for mere splendor
     or puzzlement; not to hold a candle
     to the immortal moment.
I am weary of "always." Suddenly
the shadow of the lattice is on the fountain,
reminding that of all beings, dead or undead, we
are most drowned in longing.

We will sit all day on a bench in the sun watching
    the spider monkeys.
It will at moments resemble an internal Eden.
But we will not know this.
We will think that we are just taking pictures with our minds.
The male will stand upright and scratch his silvery-gold chest.
It will sound rough and shameless.
Over and over the egg of tenderness will break in our hearts
at the sight of the baby spider monkeys.
For nothing could be more guileless or curious.
The mother will stand on all fours and stare into space
and we will see by her eyes that all of this is beyond her,
though she is intelligent she is unable to fathom
this sweet injustice nature has made cling to her back.
And we will wait for those moments
when out of the concrete slabs piled to resemble a hill
a splendidly squealing chaos of monkeys
rushes, some trespass or crime in monkeydom,
causing us to cry aloud, Look at that one!
And then also there will be those moments we are embarrassed
and only through a deliberate effort
will we not look away as the monkey
reaches backwards to pull at the indescribable
pink something that dangles from its bottom,
and we will feel our humanity is endangered
and that our intimate moments might lap over into the animal
    world
and our privacies be beheld with such ghastly frankness.
But no monkey does any one thing for very long.
So soon the candor will pass.
And gradually the shadows of the trees will touch our bench
and it will get cool, then uncomfortably cool, and there will
    be fewer
and fewer monkeys, and no one will be on the opposite bench
with detached and absorbed expression, and even the thief gulls
will have left the moat, and we will say these words as we
    stand; no;
think them: Oh God, whatever else be true, though nothing is
    permanent,
may the myth of our lives be like this memory of monkeys; that real.

§ *TEXAS SUITE*

> *"... in Dante the damned know the future*
> *but not the present."* N. FRYE

§ *1.* THE ALLNIGHT HAMBURGER
STAND IN THE DANGEROUS
NEIGHBORHOOD

The Murder Burger
is served right here.
You need not wait
at the gate of Heaven
for unleavened death.
You can be a goner
on this very corner.
Mayonnaise, onions, dominance of flesh.
If you wish to eat it
you must feed it.
"Yall come back."
"You bet."

§ 2. *THE GARAGE*

When it's night,
and the silver and black water
crawls all over itself,
and the neighbor's unfinished garage
is a boned whale in the moonlight,
and around the kerosene lantern
is a second lantern of bugs,
I take three beers onto the porch
and stretch out on the plastic lounger
to watch the Absolute
on its hands and knees in the mud.

§ 3. THE QUESTIONS

"Will I ever
Be a flame
In paint?

Will I ever
Make the brain
My T-bone steak?

Will I ever
Make of murder
Something safe?

Will the canvas
Ever yield
The Real

To me? I do not
Think I think
I will.

Will the flies
Always bejewel
My rare filet?

Will I ever
Like the weather
Drink my fill?"

§ 4.   *THE LAWN*

I lay on a quilt on the lawn
drinking my bright black Coke.
Tanya played with the dog
and Carlene with Billy Bob,
and the men sat on the porch,
three orange cigars,
and the women in aprons came to the screens,
wiping their hands like moths.

§ 5. THE CHERRIES

Cherries, blackred and wet,
glassy cleavage,
like two scars married. God
I've got a lot of cherries
yet to bury.

A cherry merchant strolling by
offered my brown dog cherry pie.
I tore a switch from the cherry tree
and it got hard.
I thought my stripped white switch would starve.

Mouths for money,
mouths for hoots,
I switched dogs
enroute, and by my wits
cornered the market
on cherry pits.

That was then.
Now I'm ripening
toward synthesis, like two feet
dancing to the tune,
Cherry Sweet, Cherry Deep, Lord
I Got Cherries Yet To Weep.

§ 6.   THE ACTUAL

I met a huge goose who walked
dripping from the little pond
straight toward me one morning
on big gold gooselegs
and the eyes of a colt and stuffed trousers.
I held out my hand: Stop! But it did
not fathom and kept coming and
I felt the chill of the Actual
nearing. Its beak was orange
and its sloping white hugeness that tapered
behind it rocked as it walked up
as tall as my belt.
I backed up, and thought: If this were a dream
it would be a nightmare. I was afraid.
What frightened me was not the goose,
but the gooseness.

§ 7.   *THE FLEA MARKET*

I.

The sun flashes on the lake
through the mimosa in which
the swallowtail butterfly pulses
like an eye in the hole of a mask.

II.

I go to the dump with my uncle and father.
O Light, mangler of cowards, placer
of the moth in the spiral,
let the rainshower fall on the cow
with the speckled haunches,
on the icily burning trash,
on the potato-colored men under the shadetree
by the pickup: "These yur gloves?"
No and Yes.

III.

My father-in-law is carving
the bust of my dead daughter in marble.
It sits on a high shelf in a houndstooth hood
like a head to be hanged.
Drink that strawberry cola, boy, that footlong ruby
in the blinding shade.
An inchworm crawls through the broom by my chair:
image of menace; could chew through the nuclear;
grandchild of a needle.
Everything south of this chair is gnats.
The juicy-rumped fly will inspect my sweetroll forever.
The cow makes milk *in* its body.
Though I knew it was a mirage,
I took my trunks. Go   Jaguars   Go,
said the bumper.

IV.

There's the sand handsome Lem
is buried in. Pity Lem, who dropped
dead in the mimosa shade, for not
even one of our sins.

V.

The woman at the flea market
with the orange juice cans
in the blown candy of her hair
sitting in the folding chair under the mimosa
said: "Then this other old gal come over
and starts a fight with this other old . . ."
Pitiful Pearl, stuffed with stockings, red thread grin. Ah,
father, these heathen christians selling hammers
and padlocks and dolls and sno cones
are parodies of men,
they eat the unplucked hens of horror, and borrow
each other's murder weapons, and their women carry
knives in their girdles to marry you with,
and they dip down into the vat of minnows
with their nets and bring up exactly
one sizzling dozen, and the concrete
issues from the nozzles of their trucks, and they pull the hose
lewdly, yanking the venom, milking the bubble
from the pump, *kick it!,* for theirs is the heathen
charity, the kindness that cleaves the violence, when it comes,
and Come It Does.

VI.

Down by the chainlink fence
the purple sixfoot irises stand,
some bulging innards through the sheaths they're in,
some dangling the old flower's rotted cloth,
sort of like Martians
pausing between gulps of human thought
to stare into my uncle's yard and
bark, boy, bark.

§ 8. THE FISHING

I.

We drag the trailer across the blacktop in the rain.
The trash is burning in the rain.
The asparagus ferns are a mass of crystal
as though the yard were holding its brain in its hands.
At night the moon
in the outhouse door
is full of stars.
You do not live in that birdhouse.
You are not that ceramic cardinal.
So stop crying.

II.

This is a partial theocracy.
A pickup with a cane in the gunrack.
Sno Ball Here.
The grief of the gravel.

III.

There must be more to this place
than the bloodweed beside the road
and the armadillo squashed out of its armor
on it.
In wholeness: the moral equivalent of the horseapple.
In candor: the rain's nudity.
There must be.

IV.

The duck has eaten the spider.
Oh.
What luck that I should witness.
No.
Cluck of the caged hen, poo-poo

of the dove, rustle of the parakeet,
rattle of the True Love Pigeon
with the forelock of gold.

V.

No one is listening.
Now you may sing the selfsong,
as the bird does, not for territory
or dominance,
but for self-enlargement.
Let something
come from nothing.
Pick up the brain by the hair and put it in the burning rain.
Make Lear wrong.

VI.

If you have nothing to say
the words never end.
"Scared to death." "Is it hot enough for you?" "Chilled to
  the bone."

VII.

I row out to the electric tower
and tie up. Night and the lake are one.
In the slip the boats
bump the nailed tires.
The small clear loneliness is mine.
Again I ache to slide from my body.
The lures lie naked in the tackle box.
I envy them. Above me the tower to which I am tied
is "singing." I slip over the edge of the boat
into the cold water and wait
for one of the gods to take me by the hair
and pull my body off me like a nightgown.

VIII.

Here lies what is left of me,
The rest is mystery.

IX.

Ignore thyself.

NEW POEMS (1983–1990)

§ SLOBTIME

I sat by the swimming pool in Port-au-Prince
watching a man whitewash a wall
with a sawed-off mop.
Most of the whitewash dripped on the dirt.
I thought, What a slob.
The waiter kept bringing me beers.
I'd been drinking since breakfast.
I didn't count.
Occasionally I'd stand up.
I did this until dusk
then ate dinner and tried to sleep.
A rooster crowed most of the night in a tree.
The next morning I ordered eggs and beer
and sat until noon making notes.
The whitewasher stood at the kitchen door
grinning at the slob on the porch.
The hotel's pet chicken
pecked at my feet for crumbs.
Don't cheat, I kept writing, Don't cheat.

No one would desire
Father to catch fire

Or Mother eat
In dark her heart

Or Cadillac
On gravel rot

Or Father by TV dissolve
Or Mother in nylon nightgown

Pridelessly walk through mud
But what can be done

To stop mask's tongue
From falling out and

Crawling across the green
Shag rug, my son?

She said it was just a catfish
but I knew bleeding breakage and waste
when I saw it, so I said to her I said,
       mmm, like a reel, mmm . . .
           and she was the texture
of Chinese beer
that evening we stood
       at the tank of minnows, I
         the shy handsome soldier
       scraping the dirt with my toe
and lying about my misfortunes
and no match for her crystallizations.
       . . . gulping, mmm, gulping
       on the floor of the boat . . .
         both of us
amazed by how long and slender
         time seemed between strokes
at midnight with the moon over us,
standing at the fish-cleaning table . . .
cloudshift making the stuck scales flush.

§ FEAR OF HOMOSEXUAL RAPE

Vision of being raped by a gang of gas station attendants.
They are holding my head down on the concrete.
They are looking for my ear in the wrong place.
I am ignorant of the fact that they are parts of a song.
Invisibility is their snake.
I mistake the sunlight for a bundle of sharpened arteries.
I throw up my hand to protect myself from my thoughts.
My holes become oysters.
Shirt unbuttoned and lace against tan chest.
The tattoos floating all over the skin.
Don't let it slide into my mouth!
After which two of them step to the iron ear
in my shorts.
Go down. The feelings are eels
soothing snails with their tongues.
The gang steps back.
Their four heads fuse into one.

§ POEM FOLLOWING DISCUSSION OF BRAIN

The dog.   The book.   The glass.
Things seen *as* things.
Arguing a theory of how we perceive. Brain
of dog discussed. The man in the catatonic state
sat up in bed when the terrier licked his face, and said,
"Where can I keep him?" First words since 1958.
Was Christ, to Lazarus, a great dane?

I argue that brain is Master
because brain is slave to Stuff.
The dog, the glass, the book,
first; *then* their transformation into images; *then*
the sensation they are standing in shimmering rings.
Even the movie credits announce
the dog playing Rex is actually King.
I eat food and brain eats names.

My friend argues for Mind minding mind's Minding.
I call that *religion.*
Without Stuff, I insist, there are no Angels.
Angels don't fall out of Heaven they crawl out of Things.
The book. The glass. The dog. Still-lifes precede drama;
just by a hair. The dog that bites you on the toe
tears off Imagination's leg.
Religion calls the dog Illusion. I call the dog
King! And he comes loping up, and licks my face,
and I wake from *and* into
dream.

§ PESSIMISM: THE BIRDS

I do not lay broken;
nothing I lay.
I prefer it this way.

Dancing is for strangers.
Everything I've said,
I've spoken. Flesh, clay—

what's the difference?
Both break. Day
is still dark when the birds start up.

That is when I lay
my head on the pillow. Cool,
unbroken.

A stranger is the prelude to a chaos.
I am passing out of contact into witness.
Blind chance makes a pattern perfect.

It's 5 a.m. I rise and read.
Heaven's a sensation.
The unanswerable birds

answer each other.
Their melody is lovely, chaos,
good to dread.

I don't dance.
I watch the dancers.
What's the difference? Try to talk.

A stranger's eyes loom large: such targets.
Heaven is assembled; made. Suavely
as a ghost of chance Time will waltz

the lonely near, and tear the skirt.
There is nothing to say
and much to tell. The birds wake up.

I'll go to Hell
a cleaving shirt
of blood and muscle, as I came.

Behold the details: fingernails,
eyelashes, veins!
Who shall claim them? The birds, perhaps.

By chance I open the book to the page
on which is written,
It is written. I prefer it this way.

They fly away.

§ JONATHAN (SAMUEL (ABNER   )
(IBID   AND HIS "LAST WORDS"

There is no way of knowing.
The sheep loathe the deer.
The fox rushes hindward, excreting a jewel.
There is no departure.
The stream copes with the stone.
More is the mercy.
The two fawns stand frozen.
Their eyes are all pupil.
For example, the Bible.
Each song spectacular & nothing is new.
The pepper is speckled.
The dogmeat uneaten.
The pig but in whispers.
The logical principle guiding the fishes.
If we cast wide our nets.
The fecund present trembles at bowlrim.
I have lost the lust of the goat in my tweeds.
His "Last Words" forgotten, the night nurse was dozing.
The salt contains rice grains to soak up the moisture.
I would pinch out the candle.
We are morsels of worship.
The hour is elastic, the lifetime a gloss.
May I punish no innocent.
He who murders his mother will always kill others.
Justice is juicy.
Mercy a lemon.
The darkness total.
After death I will go where I was before birth.
The soul in a haycart.
It will wear the black bonnet of discipline.
It will wear the throat lace and the brooch that weeps.
Down fucking & wisdom & liquid & solid.
To crack its gorged egg.
The trumpet's gold mouth will turn red.
The saxophone hung from the beard will straighten.
Then I will know my doctor, my surgeon.
For all the entities will be but events.
And the fossils will squirm in the limestone.
I will see through my flesh like saran.

These eyeballs. These teachings. These sperm.
The lure will splash and the line be invisible.
No immaculate marble, no nymph fixing sandal.
The clouds in their eulogies will lose track and vanish.
I will run the film of my life. Backwards for laughs.
The whiskers of strawberries, the clean-shaven snakes.
I will sit up suddenly in the casket's satin.
The moment, the hung dot, the cough in the audience.
I have worn out my welcome.
Take my ring and my nose.
The brain is a furnace.
Is transformed and transforms.
I have soiled my solo.
In midair the lit dust is swimming.
Ten thousand times random and then once a Rose.
To the does the meek sheep seem savage.
Mostly it's music.
The cello is oxblood.
It is no sin that the skin fits so tightly.
He is stiff, but a candle.
Unnamed goes the embryo.
How many eyeballs to fill this straw hamper?
The jellyfish dangle.
Unlucky chameleon, lime green in black cat.
You are dead but don't know it, he said. Yet I heard him.
I gave God a lamb but He spat it out.
That was pre-logic.
Which is why I was born.
May my dog not avenge me.
The piano is open. The strings gleam in the lid.
Its lacquer looks famished. Gorged,
I climb in.

Think of them, praising songbirds and peonies
in one line and warriors
spear-split from throat to balls in the next, Spring
as old as ever, new to them, mace
gory, corpses among the wild dill
and iceplants, those who died ten times in a day,
and got up in the morning to water the houseplants,
eyes sparkling with sanity & madness, that cleansing
paradox, "I died! I'm alive! I earned it!"

I called the Cow
and she came to me,
black and brown, she bowed
her smooth blunt head, and said,
"I am one of the dead,
who come and go like flowers,
who rarely speak your tongue,
and so you think us dumb
beasts, but we are not so,
we are trapped between death and life,
unable to want, or choose,
I have no dread, I have no name,
all my faces are the same
black or brown, with blaze,
I eat, I drink, I stand
in the shade of the one shade tree
and try, like flames, to *think*."

S HE WHO WAITS

I looked down, naked, from room 310
of the Royal Orleans Hotel, at the
magnolia trees. It was night, no streetlamps near,
the enormous white waxy magnolias hanging
like skulls in the greenblack leaves.
Anne was in the garage getting Tabs from the drink machine
and Chris was with her. I pulled back
the gauze curtain,
and stood there waiting, as always,
for some event, in energy, in matter, in psychology,
in what *exceeds*,
to open my skull cap, grasp my brain
and place it, beating, on the table
between the two chairs and the hanging lamp.

When the palm tree
flowers
it is like no other
flowering thing.
There is trouble ahead.
Straight up from this god
forsaken oasis
Las Vegas the white
flowers of the palm tree
blow down and float
in the hotel pool.
It is the third stage
of life, and it is desperate.
It can have no happy ending.
It can have no happy middle.
We thought they were like
the ferns, sexless spores
along the long leaves' spines.
Then this. We look up. We are not prepared.
A pompom of flowerlets
shakes down in the furnace air
onto the cold pool
its litter
of sperm.

§ THE SCAPEGOAT

A scapegoat is what we need.
What is this scapegoat to be? Will it be
iridescent, feathered? A grunt
on the hoof? Will it be flesh
and knowledge? Whatever the squealing thing is
which must be hogtied and bled dry and smoked,
let it come now. For we do most desperately need a scapegoat.
The Jew would do; but he is used up.
The nigger won't do. He has no goat. The queer is nearly
perfect, but too dispersed; and there aren't enough.
Women? No. Too many to blame; and anyway
many of them are Us.
We need a goat that will fit the flame of our daily roast
more neatly.
And if we do not find this scapegoat soon we shall go insane.
And if we go insane, again,
we'll slit each other, from here to here, and hallucinate
spiders of blood in our beer;
and that wouldn't do. Besides,
that's the scapegoat's fate. We must take the intensity
of the hate we feel as proof of God's will; and cooperate.
Please do not donate your sacred cow.
We must get one thing straight:
this is no charity; this is slaughter of fear.
We must root from our minds these last two decades
of polarization, and sexual violence, and political corruption,
and national self-doubt, and
you name it, pal. I can see it now. A scapegoat
whose wounds the bayonet fits
like a tongue does a mouth.
Who screams in a gibberish language. Like, say,
Arabic, Atheist, Art.
We must name the fiend Fiend and then root the fiend out.
Or the boat that's been rocked might sink.
One more assassination might do it. One more rape.
Name your Top Ten, and from these a panel will choose.
The pornographer. The pederast. The fetus. The nude.
Who is this scapegoat to be? Maybe
you? Spread your legs. Wider. Bend over. Moo.

I loved my madness
but it wrecked my car,
and threw me through the windshield,
and the windshield was real,
but I lived,
and my madness pretended to suffer death,
so I buried him under
the pear tree, the pear tree in my head,
my face was all carved up,
and chickenblood spewed on the road,
roosters of chickenblood,
but I put my face
back in place, it was changed
but still mine,
and the paramedic offered me wine,
but I said No, wine
drives me mad, and his white coat
burst open with numerous
female breasts, each
squirting milk, and I said
No thanks, my god
you look soft, but
it would be mad to drink
from you, and the breasts
changed into penises,
and each penis was mine,
but I only had two hands,
for which I was glad, so I got
out of the ambulance and stood
at the roadside with my thumb
stuck out, and a stranger stopped,
stranger than most, so
I didn't get in, and he said
What's the matter? And I said
it would be mad to do this,
and then it got dark and it rained,
so I walked into the nearby town,
and had some coffee and cherry pie
at the counter, where the local cops
bragged about scaring the shit

out of this driver and that, and I said
Officer, I just crawled from a wreck,
just look at my shirt (it was stiff
with blood), and the blond one said,
Are you crazy, I'm on my break,
so I threw the hot coffee
in his face, and he dropped
to his knees and began to beg, and
said, Forgive me, Forgive me, now
I understand, and I walked outside
and the rain had stopped and the ribbon
of blacktop shined to my right and my left,
and I knew I had outlived madness,
and it made me feel a little sad, but
I got a ride in a Cadillac with a nice
old man with silver hair who disliked talk, so I
crawled into the back and all the way to LA slept
the sleep of those no longer mad.

§ MADNESS: FULLGROWN

1.

Madness,
now,
lie down,
lie down,
your extremes
have been excellent,
now you must lay
your thorn crown
in the snow.
Take your dread,
take your cane,
pick up your pride and your brain
and go.

2.

Over the snow
white snow I saw
Madness in silhouette
gnawing a bone.
And the wolves
crouched and moaned,
and the does stood
still by their
stark still fawns,
and the sea-egrets came
to the fresh water creek
in the woods,
to drink,
and Madness looked on
at the sane incoherence
of vine leaf & seed,
then crept off
alone, to weep.

3.

Each man and each woman lay,
lover to lover, in the roofless dark,
in and out, in and out, like a heart
makes its moves, and the springs
creaked in unison and the shoes
on the floor by the fire
approved. Madness, I said,
We have been, we have done.
What you have given is what I've outgrown.
Now, blow the coals gold.
And throw my old skin in the stove
as you go.

The rain of reason, will it come.
Will the thief be reasonable
and eat what he steals. Is there
a long brown hair
in the mayonnaise.
Does the lithograph holstein *know*.
A snowflake crushes the skull
of the beast in the ditch
with the bloodshot eyes.
Will the bum in the crusty thongs
be served. No, they show him the door.
The cat climbs the drape. The raccoon
locked in the guest-house goes mad.
Will reason rise and its net of rain
darken and crackle and fall.

I told them
when he said
the room's too yellow
you are no eagle
or Trojan band
gold is not squealing
in your basket
of trout
silver is.

§ AFTER MASSACRE

1.

Puff up, lily.

And I will pretend you are an allegory
    of beings blowing their brains out
    for the veins in a petal. For that much
    order.

2.

I predict each lily will
be a white lily.

3.

Pull the dead out by the ankles.
It has been five days. Against the stench
wear the vinegar-soaked handkerchief.
These were my friends, some of whom I hated.
Rake up the viscera. Put it in a basket.
Say the same things over and over.
Have the same memories. Tell the same lies.
Look, over there,
in the sweet william,
a head.

Mom this morning received by Federal Express the script
of her movie The Vampire Lestat.
She is sitting in the bedroom with the door
mostly closed. I saw only a few words:
"Open on Akasha's eyes, 'in-close.' "
Yesterday morning and this morning the shower water went
ice-cold. And last night the washing machine
began to smoke and smell of burnt rubber.
Christopher put his one free hand and his crossword puzzle
book to his ears and went into the other room.
Christopher was afraid the smoke alarm would go off.
I got the front panel loose and looked inside.
The motor was
many wrappings of beautiful copper wire.
There is a style here which is very interesting.
The women wear their hair long which they pin back with
plastic barrettes shaped like bows. They shave their eyebrows off
then draw them back on as thin pencil lines. They look
like masks
of little girls.
They were
enjoying the feeling.
I'm waiting for the washing machine repairman.
He says he probably doesn't have the part but he is coming
from Trinidad.
No one ever shows up on time.
Since the leaves have all fallen I can see
the lake.
I guess Mom and I will have to put in a new water
heater.
They say this weekend frozen rain
will fall.
After we had finished our cheeseburgers a man came up to our
table and asked my father "Did you say Bill Kelly died?"
The waitress wears very tight jeans. If she were a man
she would scream.
Under the swingset, or on the ashpile.
Mom just came in and said the script was Junk.
I held my temples.
"I've heard enough!"

She is walking around in her nightgown wondering whom to
kill. Script
writers are not writers. They are carvers of skeletons.
Christopher is walking back and forth on the linoleum in his
new cowboy boots chewing gum. The boots are made out of
rubber. Dad thinks these
will last about three weeks.
Three years ago here there struck
a powerful ice storm. The water supply went out. For two
weeks no one could flush a toilet. They could not
get buckets of water from the lake because the lake was
frozen. Big Dad and Big Mother had pneumonia and flu.
Christopher just spelled "mojave" correctly, which Mom
always calls the mo-jave, as in no-slave. Dad calls
the gas stations there Pit Stops In Hell.
When the ice storm came
people were kind to each other.
Sister brought water from Dallas
in every conceivable container.
At that time she did not have this Jaguar which she has lent me.
Maybe we should wash these transparent drapes.
If you do not operate a washing machine for 5 years when you
turn it on the chances are it will break.
There is a Pontiac under this house.
It is a slope up and a slope down of dust.
Only the tires show. They are nearly flat.
It is greatly instructive to pretend to be tentative. This
makes each small thing monumental.
Last night we ate at Catfish Corner.
They batter them in breadcrumbs.
Catfish are scavengers.
So you are eating what has lived its life
on garbage and carrion.
I thought about mentioning this at dinner
but decided to be tentative.
The girl at the 7-Eleven had to go into the back
to get a six pack of refrigerated Tab.
Mom said, "It's like you're going to the coal mine."
and the girl said
"It's cold ok."

No one ever drives down our road
so if someone does today I can presume it is the washing machine
repairman.
Christopher says he can't eat *all* of the chocolate covered
cherries.
Mom reminds him there is no law that he must.
When you are tentative
you can behave very naively toward the most mundane things.
The recliner will no longer vibrate.
The repairman said he would come Around Lunchtime.
I did not ask him when he ate lunch.
Mom says the scriptwriter has included none of the mythology.
Dad bangs his palm against his temple.
It makes no difference to Christopher that his boots
are rubber.
It would bother me a lot.
I am a purist.
The Dallas-Fort Worth area
calls itself The Metroplex.
This is a copyrighted term and no other cities
may call themselves this.
Dallas could be a city on Venus.
What did the volunteer fireman who put up this new wall paneling
do with the pictures I had hanging?
This fake grasspaper is so naked.
It is not clear when autobiographical data should be suppressed.
No one lives forever.
The dream was so sexually arousing I thought I had a third hand.
This evening we ate dinner at a bar-b-cue place owned by a man
with the first name of Schraft. I told
Big Dad
that sounded like the name of a science fiction
character.
Schraft of Gormlon.
We laughed.
At a table near the cash register was sitting
a bearded young man wearing a huge black
cowboy hat and the name BUBBA tattooed on his arm.
Bubba was the boy friend of the cashier.
On a far wooden table was a TV on which was

The Dating Game.
Everything was exquisitely
appropriate.
Outside, the tiny cold mist fell on Gun Barrel City.
I explained to Big Mother and Big Dad
how a disruption in biogenic amines
can short-circuit the electro-chemical
activity among the neurons of the brain
and cause loss of memory.
Big Dad said he could be talking along
and then not be able to come up with the noun
of the sentence, For example, Would you hand me that . . .
and he could not say "screwdriver."
It was a moment of sorrow.
The repairman had not in 14 years
of working on washing machines
seen one chew up its own splashguard.
I did not crack up.
Christopher was sure he saw a poster
for the Texas Chainsaw Massacre in the window
of Movies Unltd.
So we drove by very slowly
while he covered his head with his coat.
I entertained the idea
of looking up at a perfectly square moon.
This was silly.
The night was moonless.
An ice storm is predicted.
I must nail up the longhorn horns.
Perhaps soon he will be able to remember both the nouns and the
verbs.
Then I will have to imagine him "my shrine of blood."
As all old things
wink out, slurring the candle, squaring the moon, bobbing
the empty rowboat.
I assured Big Dad that according
to what I had seen on TV they do NOT
break your ribs to get to your heart.
I could tell his curiosity was serious.
Once home we all ate Blue Bell Homestyle Vanilla.

Sister has called to ask me
to take the film out of the trunk
so it wouldn't freeze.
This leads to a very delicate moment
in the cold mist training all my attention
on the logic of a ring of strange keys.
The only other things in the trunk
were a Gumby telephone and tiretools.
We all ate our ice cream in silence.
How is it possible to know when to stop remembering things?
Since it is Saturday
we go in to the
Mall. Everything in Homer, all the
wine dark sea, the whale road, the frozen
grass of Horace, Plato's paradise of ideal
tables and raincoats, these plethora,
erupt into physical being in the Mall. We behold
our
buried dead formally stating their case.
The beauty and safety of the Mall is our forefathers' gift.
First we look for books. Then we look for leather jackets.
Then we have coffee on the glass tables
outside Nieman's. The ice cold air blows our hair.
We look for televisions in Joskes.
The sun is setting but we are immune.
We
go down into
manpower, humor, debt. We look at shirts.
We buy shirts. This is the moment
the flint knife digs out
the jumping heart of the sacrifice
slave. Then we sit calmly on the lip of the planter,
fulfilled. I ask Big Dad
does he believe God created it all.
He says Adam and Eve is a myth.
Big Mother astonishes me a great deal by saying
"The older I get the more explanation I need."
It is a very simple moment.
The ice storm still has not reached us.
We drive home in the headlight illuminated rain with

the stuff in the trunk.
Tomorrow it will be Sunday
in middle America.
That is not just a phrase.
People will look up at the stunt planes
in the clear opal everywhere
except for the red smoke
they trail. The children
will be potato white
or as black as syrup
with their newly minted parents in cameo.
No theme
can trick memory. It has its own pattern.
This is more stupefying than the placement of galaxies.
Though the law *is* the law.
Some will foolishly place the paper
cup of beer on the living blanket.
This is all in the future tense
because although it is an eternal verity
it has not happened yet.
It is like the crepe myrtle in winter.
After the hailstorm
the trees were leafless.
It was not possible to say this would happen.
It does not figure.
The dog that *bites* everyone else
brings this one stranger
its rubber porkchop.
All the sales people
mention the approaching storm.
Homer's grey gods
strolling the fields of slaughter
stoop to pick up the choking child in the stroller.
Is this less eternal than that?
The weather is greater than we.
We love being reminded that we are children.
We drive home at night in the rain
with the brass lamp in its plastic bag in the trunk.
Mom is silent, suffering the script.
Christopher's head is on my shoulder.

Big Dad is weaving in and out of his lane
and we do not know why.
For 40 years I have looked at the back of that head.
Mom sits like a doll under the quilted chicken.
The stupid script
lies open in her lap.
It is like nothing.
It is out of her hands.
She knew this moment would come.
I dread returning to the actual world.
In the Department Store
thirty TVs were tuned to the same basketball game.
But I digress.
There is no designer
but there is a design.
There is no watchmaker
but there is a watch.
Morning again. Mockingbird's
liquid immediacy, colloquial.
I put on my pants, oh!, It feels like I'm stepping in water!
The goldtailed
squirrel puts its hand to its face.
The autumn leaves
on the base of the lamp never
fall, are always falling.
I take the nursery rhyme
into the slaughter house.
Shoveling the shambles into my
clown cup. Greensleeves is on the blaster.
Steam from the glassy coffee. The Japanese
disaster-bird bites at its own yellow feet
for possessing the branch:
Style over Substance. The derangement
of the age.
Maybe today I will go down
to see if more ducks have hatched
in my boat.
To see
how thick the spider webs are on the steering wheel.
Do they eat them? God knows no decay is wasted.

Striding over the naked and beheaded soldiers,
grey as a raincloud, Homer's
woman.
Pretty soon we will cross the street
to Big Mother's for turkey.
Pine's spiked rain-spangled brain still black.
I get into a vigorous argument
with Sister's Husband
about whether employers have the right
to demand that their employees submit
to drug test urinalysis.
Big Mother gets frightened when we raise our voices.
We have eaten our ice cream.
He thinks one's civil rights
can be selectively violated if
the thing stamped out is
Really Bad.
Then we talk about faith healing.
Then I notice the red geraniums in the window box
outside
are artificial geraniums.
There is a knock at the door.
It is the police.
They stand in the grey east
with needles. They wear bandilleros
with empty test tubes
where the bullets should fit.
They are the bosses. They are authority.
They order each of us to stand up and piss.
God damned green time.
A dieting woman
is no one to joke with.
Christ ate catfish with Bubba in Gun Barrel City.
This morning there was no hot water again.
And the hot water heater is *new.*
I lean on the oak stick of death.
Above us the thicket of stars.
Uncle waxes his truck. $16,000
to have the concrete garage floor poured.
After 31 years with that company

Uncle was axed. Oil fell to $8 a barrel.
So Uncle walks down to the lake
carrying the oak stick of death.
It isn't his. It's borrowed.
His neck is bent. His wife is under water.
Moon drops
tangerine from the thunderhead.
Christopher goes from chair to chair.
Big Dad goes into Dallas
for an angiogram.
So who, she asks, has got
30 thousand dollars for a bypass? Us?
Handling Uncle is delicate.
Even when discussing the water heater
he is the mask of tragedy.
The leafless tree's blood veins
are clotted with mistletoe.
The yellow hovel standing alone says FIREWORKS.
People live in silver trailers.
Some of us are peasants.
The hunk of copper they brought back from Solomon's Mines
they glue to the wall of their variety store.
Satan tempts us with sex. Those are his lyrics.
His snakeskin goes platinum.
If it weren't for rust, some of us
would *never* work.
My brother was stationed in Monterey
and I nearly froze, she said. She is from the lust bowl.
If it doesn't work, kick it.
They have a Camaro but no electricity.
The first store sells shoes and popcorn.
The second sells antiques and ice cream with tea.
These are not paradoxical.
Variety is the logic of sex.
The lake is sinfully blue.
From the porch eave hung the cat-fangs of ice.
They looked inevitable
but skill had nothing to do with it.
Now we are going to Town East

to buy Step-Grandmother a piece of cut crystal
if they have cut crystal in Sears.
I see my father cross the St. Augustine to his truck.
I must prove this.
Holding his keys, as though they were heavy.
Is there more than the light-encrusted
curvature of the Earth.
Is there a black line
drawn in the dirt you can step over then come back across.
Change, and all its leaves, and all its dead sticks.
What are those lights out there?
Towns In The Distance.
He is putting his first foot down by the ceramic frog
and walking again as above.
The truck door slams but No Sound.
I try to dream him up.
I don't like this dream.
What does it prove.
The car's headlights move through the roadside weeds
like the lamp of a scuba diver.
Something nearing takes shape before form.
What are those lights out there?
"I don't know. Towns in the distance."
She leaves the cellophane on her lampshades.
The peasantry is rich enough
to afford head-cheese linoleum.
BUY.SELL.TRADE.
Lights of the towns in the distance
as though where the turning sky
scraped off its stars.
Then the long stretch of field is blacker than the heavens.
That is the line in the dirt.
Big Dad, walking toward it.
Though the tone wanders
the intent is song.
Sometimes it may sound like the cowboy song of a child.
The washing machine works now.
We were faithful to our senses.
The real is ideal.

Yesterday we went to Wal-Mart and bought
a microwave oven, a tape radio player, a
blender, a coffee maker, dishes for four, a machete,
and $495.00 worth of miscellaneous stuff, and
the salesgirl said,
"What *happened,* did *you* guys have a *fire?*"

§ WALKING WITH MY SON TO THE CREEK IN THE DARK WHICH HE FEARS

Oh little boy   grief fleshed out
coming along   after the owl
has lifted the mouse   from the azure slab
put on your red hood   and walk with me in the yard
of crushed gravel   under the stars
we two noiseless people   and you just a child.
Are you cold?   I tighten the hoodstring.
We come to the creek   in the darkness
and across it   the iron woods
containing whatever your mind   puts in it
which you fear
as though thoughts   were as real as animals
which   whatever their powers
they aren't   I tell you this over and over
but don't ask   your mother
for she   is your mother
I have the flashlight   I have the gun
and the knife   I am the father
the darkness to me   is not over-imagined
you and   your mother
are similar   that way
are you cold?   I know you don't like poems
but in one poem   I love
across a river like this   except in bright daylight
a man's daughter   jumped up and down
and he called her   his pearl without spot
only she   was dead
and it was   the river of death
so he couldn't reach her   ever
and it broke my heart.   Then you were born
a boy   no less
and alive   not across some river
of booze or grass or the grave   I saw this in my mind
for my mind also   can fill in the blanks with monsters
as yours does   the black iron woods
with monsters   my monsters
I do not fear nothing
I think I expected you   to dispel
blow them away   like smoke in our fireplace

but what could you do   you were a child
and had no power   over the powers of death.
Here   let me tie that string tighter.
And every time I looked up   there was a wood
in daylight   an immediate pitiless daylight
and you and your mother   were in it
holding hands   of the same habits of mind
the same fears   and obsessions
and I was afraid   of you
both   and said to myself
about you   are you without spot?
What a thing for a man   to ask of a child
his own son   whom he does not want
to fear the dark   yet when he does fear it I think
she went into death   into the light
that roasts   and blackens the pearl
so who are you   and who is your mother
to be such lovers   while my lover
jumps up and down   in a poem in a field in a book.
So we go   as far as we dare go tonight
not into   the woods that scare you
you and I   a father and his little boy
nine years old   of whom I ask
more than I ask of myself,   a man
as afraid   of climbing
this slope of black moments   as you
who cannot save me   but will.

There it is. Each thing.
Were it not beautiful
It would be invisible.
Even death, and its preferences.
Salt rock & lightwave.
Eels on the creamy seabottom.
Snow held by branch in balance.
Some suffering unbearable, borne.
The snowcrust lives on in the shade.
No matter matter. Or the weightless idea.
Where else but uterus
Which is galaxy's proxy.
Spider, personless. Prey, pure.
Each leg with its own brain
Arousing the ovaries to rapture,
Rupture. Shapely the aftermath.
Death gags on its masterpiece.
The seed of the apple of the eye
Pierces the pupil. The sapling
Unwrinkles its branches in brain.
Death's tongue retracts
From the uterus. Uselessly
Hangs from the hair. Of the lips.
Of the lover. Of the murder.
That backfired. Each nerve
In concert, alert. As foetus,
Fatal. The dog treats its bone
As though the bone had a soul.
If it were not beautiful
We could not see it.
In the light of morning.
In the dazzling interior sapling.
There it is.

Dominance. Is it natural?
Slavery. Is it natural?
Pre-dynastic Egypt
baboon mummy wrapped in brown gauze
now looks like iron. Is it natural?
Chop off the bread-thief's hand.
Is it not logic? Do not some deaths
make us feel better?
Has the slasher been punished?
No, not imprisoned. *Punished.*
Is violence necessary? Violence.
Is it as good for the goose as the gander?
Is this a purgative? Oratory
of mynabird? Inevitable
monstrous two-toned limousine of cancer?

§ 20 GALLON AQUARIUM

The awesome forms of thought become
the silver goldfish one by one.
Their gauze fins fan the fluorescent light
and move the weeds from left to right.
Their bloodred foreheads bump the glass.
Down from their little Heaven Above
the large slow flakes of food descend.
They gulp the given off black gravel. At one end,
the awesome source of all their assumptions
humms & bubbles.

The iceplants
turn to the sun
their purple
sadist flowers.
To the water
returns the water.
To the curvature
the tanker.
Every form
in some dimension.
Scope resolves
the blurred departure.
To the skillet
returns the fish
and the finger
to the roster.

§ NOTE TO EZRA

Well, Ezra,
goat,
they have gutted
the lute,

now they say
the experience
of King Lear
is no more than
"playing with forms,"

and they have hung
the lute's guts
in icewater,

merely
        "playing with forms,"

digging in the dirt in the dark
for the silver vulvas of figs,

saying,   Oh never mind
        it's just a tube
        of naples yellow
        I stepped on

and not the vagina of Helen.

§ THE DOCTRINE OF PERCEPTION AS ANIMAL HUNGER

——which is an extension of the doctrine of the Rattlesnake
touching Tarantula reared back on its tiptoes and
rowing its long front legs and the
oxblood black tongue in-and-out.

——which is an extension of the doctrine of the Kangaroo Rat
meeting the Kangaroo Rat in their mutual escape route
and poking its head through the sandgrains that crumble to
illuminate
the little eyes brightly as ink-drops.

——which is an extension of the doctrine of the Very Little
Differences
that precede "splendor", or
life as Roasted Light, water alone,
or Morandi's wooden bottles emerging in negative whiteness
as emotional algebra, smooth and discrete.

——which is an extension of the doctrine of the Gravitational
Equilibrium of the Buddha sitting
in a zero, gold torso, blue trousers, babyfat,
which places perception again in Athens, the ugly,
about to open the door of the National Museum
on the cocktail party of soapwhite people and jockeys,
stopped.

——which is an extension of the doctrine of the Sun
on the snowman's frozen-shelled skull of crumbling and melting
glass-grains losing its eyeballs to inwardness.

——which is the doctrine of love as Cannibal Tenderness,
the eagle ascends, in its talons hanging below it like an
umbilicus
the black squiggle of Rattlesnake, poor baby, poor
puss.

——which is the doctrine of Autobiography taken to the limit
of animal order, which is the self-centered leaping and cuteness

of the Kangaroo Rat immediately preceding the snake's
fang-cunt of Death.

——which is an extension of the doctrine of the chaos
of the minnows sizzling in the tank of oxygenated
water in the yellow lightbulbed shed attached
to the gas station foodstore, which is
the empowerment of the senses, sentiments, statements,
which is the engorgement of the ditch with itself

and the doctrine of perception as animal hunger defined.

Rhoda presumes.
Paul pulls the beard. Zack
is puzzled. Marvin grimly
mows the lawn, then the gravel.
Lydia, Lydia, of the gold down.
Dennis the drunkard.
Morgan ejaculates. Tanya
is mordant. Art
mimics Arthur. Frank
nods off in the door length mirror.
Howie joins him. Rita
hangs by a thread
from the iron gaze of William.
Who is cheeked like the cherry.
James, the blameless. Joyce
of the oyster.
Anita who cannot not talk.
Samuel who cannot talk.
Christine adjudicates. Patricia
prepares her next need.
Carlene the dark. Elizabeth the hairless.
Ellen the maker of only white meals.
Ellen the bone-white. George,
who was rich. Juliette the hesitant.
Dick finishing her sentences. Theodore taking
the two hour shower.
Brenda's sincerity. Kathleen, Kathleen,
the meat-eating flower. Frederick the feminine.
Sarge, the non-human.
John over-tips. Lisa repeatedly marries,
demarries. Ruth over-stays. Rose is raw. Robert gourmands.
Natalie sighs. Stanley, our hero,
blah, blah, blah.

I will focus on the commonplace miracle.
Even at this moment the milkcows of India.
The worm's length can exceed its own need but no more.
Wet life drying out spills the sun's entrails.
The cowskull offers the wasps its spinehole to nest in.
As useless as tits on a bull.
I will make of autobiography a roast pig
whose glazed and tightened skin,
implying that the art of our age has failed us,
oozes.
This little morsel, this mooing mind.
The turnip's blood menaces no sponges.
We are invited by cows into the chaos before milk.
Having been lured into the belief that the pile of spilled sugar
is where the ghost eased its bowels.
Not that ground glass
should salt the condom.
Each thing comes in its clothes to the roast.
Voices in chorus imply the ego
wordlessly eating its hay.
I, who am troubled by symmetry, whether to loathe it
or make it my god.
We wait at graveside for the clichés and umbrellas.
Who knows what words want of things?
Not I, master.
So I swallow the key.

We are in an oceanside
restaurant
and

the late dusk
first planet
shines headlight white

in the place the green
turns purple
and below us

the waves become white and then vanish
and far out
on the sliding black mercury

water
a freighter's
lightbulbs

fill
the known
world.

§ *LOCAL DEITY*

Bahnt-sud-i-ahm, in the now purple-leafed
plum tree, moving sensibly in the breeze,
next to the aloof Hangman Peach, which recently went
from naked, to flowered, to this, and next to it
the Van Gogh spruce,
black in its twisted middle,
    Bahnt-sud-i-ahm, maker
of the ice cream breasted dove, that shitmachine,
of the nylon rainbow octopus windsock and its lunatic shadow,
of the spool table that still oozes resin
(it makes me think of a diva clearing her throat),

    my house is your house.

S NDAAYA

I.

Ndaaya's husband has deserted her. Now, childless and husbandless, she is scorned by the other women as a worthless widow, by the men as an available whore, and by both as a freak. Her husband is called Ribs-showing.

> Broom comes to rubbish,
> rubbish to broom—
> The song-bird flees
> where death strikes twice—
> If I could be born a thousand more times
> not once would I wish it to be
> as a woman—
> "Worn stirring stick"—
> Now I am sterile—
> Ribs-showing is dead, Like-the-dead, Good-as-dead—
> So I am called Chicken-in-the-dark,
> the "talkative"—
> My feet boil, my leg muscles know—
> It is men's affair
> this killing and war—
> If I were a man I would lift this pestle—
> My nephew
> as hard as the dirt path to the river—
> I cry these laments for him
> but they are for my daughter, too,
> because it is permitted for griefs to mix—
> Being twice abandoned, I am nothing to them—
> So I will stuff my soul's double in a scarf
> and my womb in the waterjar—
> Wife, mother, sister—now any-man's chicken—
> I avert my eyes
> and stare at the dust
> —lest they read my mind.

2.

*Ndaaya's daughter and nephew have died in the same year. She blames
the sorcerer for both deaths. Having been called to join the ritual
grieving for her little nephew, she reluctantly agrees to travel to her
sister's house in a neighboring village.*

Those eyeglasses, like someone has spit in your face,
that silver hair, you godless sorcerer,
this is the second death of a child in my house
this year—
if I flopped down and cried out Beeleebelee! Beeleebelee!
what god would make
the bones happy again?
So I swallow my anger, avoid the market, withdraw
like a snail fooled by mist—
my nephew: hard as tourist-wood!
I am too proud to flop down for such satisfied gods,
for such illusions.
We women
might as well give birth
squatting over a new-dug grave;
save time, money, rags.
If you were not my sister I would say Let Death
keep the path between our houses smooth:
     He knows the way.

3.

*She knows that to venture out to her sister's house is dangerous. The
sorcerer, whom she has publicly mocked, is her enemy. "Crossroads"—
it is tempting fate to stand where others have deposited the illnesses
and evils of which they have been cleansed.*

Death-smoothed path,
Weeds beaten down,
To my sister's house,
Follow one and you come to water,
The other to humps of graves.

The moon, its light is like ashes.
When I was a mother
I felt the milk coming, I glistened.
Fill a quart jar with your tears:
The dead stay dead.
If she were not my sister
Who could get me out of my house like this
To be scoffed at?
Oh Mother, your headscarf became rotten,
Scooped from Repulsive River,
So slimy the cattle won't drink from it.
The mamba crawls over the whetstone.
I squat to piss at the crossroads
Where others have deposited the evils
Of which they were cleansed.
And the dust runs with gold for a moment.

4.

Ndaaya travels on to her sister's house. She laments her fate as a woman and considers with loathing the spiteful accusations of all those who despise her. When a male dies, the men accuse the women of sorcery.

Stretched over the maternal toilet,
this nest of hairs, ugh,
I did not make the place life comes from
yet share the blame in their minds
with the yanked up yam.
Shake the shells for your Mother
who was born a bone-needle with brains.
Ah, brothers, for you it is easy.
You steal away, live on raw tuna,
play the gazelle with your town-cunts,
while my stool gets encrusted
and time's sand makes an anthill.
When moles make the rootbed seethe
who is sent out with a sharp stick to kill them,
You?
Your woman.

Now my name is whispered, ". . . she there,
chicken-after-dark . . ."
They say the songbird has left my roof,
its feet tangled in thread.
Everything is ritual, everything.
And because I am childless,
my daughter in her short grave, Ribs-showing
who-knows-where, in a town
hauling buckets from Repulsive River,
hoping diamonds will plug up his sieve.
And if I even show my face in daylight
men stare and say "yum" and say "sorcery".
My womb is turned inside out and
the pointing women whisper "pig-bladder".
It is forbidden to imagine better things,
it is forbidden to imagine better things.
But I am lucky to be so abandoned, yes
now I have permission to be a chicken, a stray goat,
sterile as a slit drum, my facebones stick out
my breasts are as flat as the Land-Rover's waterbags.
YOU struck my mother and *I* am the one accused
of sorcery, what a laugh, I laugh and laugh, to be born
a woman, to be the crushed cricket
blamed for the shortage of food.

5.

*Halfway to her sister's house she comes to the River-of-Life-and-Death.
On the other bank the Dead beckon to her. She bends over and shows
them her privates and their hearts break and they cry out "Bee-beel-ee-
beel-ee!"*

I can out-stare the snake,
I can pierce the familiar
and open the unknown,
that gristle and smoothness,
taking on voice and face.
Footsteps need not make footprints.
I approach the stream where the feather was lost.

The dead see me, I bend over, they gaze
in mock horror
at the Queen of Cracks, licking
the air, stiff on the other streambank,
those freckled albinos.
I turn over the rock and show myself to the salamander.
Fast he squirts into the moist
rotted wood's
softness.
I am softer.
The Dead feel me as though I were a cottonseed in a quilt.
But tears come to my eyes. Things alter,
human things.
What snake weeps
after it has
swallowed the blinking frog and vomited the bones?
The hairs stand on end. Little daughter, nephew,
smelly porridge.
I lift my skirt and bend over.
The Dead groan on the opposite streambank
for a whiff of what
I have shown them.

6.

Ndaaya knows she is stronger than the cowardly men, than the false
sorcerer. But she is trapped in a woman's body, and in what is forbidden
to her. The husband's mother's spirit resides in a tree planted by the
son and tended by the first wife. She arrives at her sister's house.

Human things change.
Images are what
I nag the world of dead men with.
So they cannot dismiss what I say
as mere bitching.
If I reach into their spleens
and pull the infant ghost, shaking it,
you liars, look at what is left us
who stirred your porridge, a "talkative" woman.

Vain males saying they were leopard-brothers,
now their heads lie unburied, separately.
I would carry the shade-tree-of-my-mother-in-law
in my scarf to the sorcerer
who wears eyeglasses like someone spit in his face,
saying, I urinate on this ju-ju, so what?
And he throws the bones and I say,
You wanted a bar to sell English gin
built in the grotto but first had to clean out
the vampire bats and the new asphalt road
to the graveyard cracked in the first rainy season—
Fuck your bones!
Human things change, the cows from the model cattle farm
are the bar's only patrons.
I laugh, my marriage is broken, why should I go on
watering this tree?
I project myself as a man, a hunter, away from
these hissing women, these superior women.
As a man I approach, as a singer. Let them hiss
that no woman should sing, should make histories.
But then I must hush, lest they read my mind.
As I approach my sister's house, already, again,
just one more bee at the hole in the female tree.

7.

She goes out for firewood and thinks of the Dead and what they crave.

Stiff, stiff.
Wet, wet.
Spider does not stick to her own web.
Otherness animates the world.
If chased
the heart can dig down, kicking back dirt like a trapdoor wasp,
if dread nears, blowing smoke on its helmeted head.
Fish, fish.
Odor of my soul.
The dead stand on the other bank
prodding each other with reeds.

Their hearts are somewhere else and they know it.
They weep that every songbird has a twin,
one in my world and one in theirs
and theirs doesn't sing.
I fill my scarf with mushrooms.
They make no noise when pulled.
Their sisters poke up in hairless innocence.
More's the pity.
The leopards mate,
the female rolls over and slashes him
then re-offers herself.
When broken open the penis-shaped mushroom reveals
the vaginas inside it.
Though the snake seems neckless
the mongoose finds it.
I return to my sister's house with firewood,
clapping two sticks together
to warn the Others that a human is passing,
an equal.

8.

*Returning from gathering firewood Ndaaya is overcome by an almost
suicidal despair. She hallucinates herself as a hooded and voiceless
ghost.*

A rag is thrown over my head.
No eyeholes are cut in it.
So I am a bag with a voice.
Daughter dead, nephew dead, Ribs-showing
maybe in the marble river
of Islam.
Eyes painted on rag never blink.
She is I but not me.
Children avoid my path.
Sleep is a punishment.
The stream that once spoke my language of images
babbles like tree-monkeys
who think every speckled flower a leopard.

To sing and to mean need not be the same.
A rag can have a painted mouth
and my vulva opens and closes like a hippo's nostril.
Things have happened, human things.
Death has stopped at the crossroads to talk with the ants.
Tell me about joy.
Tell this rag hood about that.

9.

She remembers how at her daughter's death she suffered a similar trance of madness but was made sane by her capacity for song.

I lay down, fluttering.
My eyes became mostly white.
The nettles are still alive
but my daughter, my healthy daughter
born with gums strong as cut teeth,
lies hardening and curling
like dung.
Instantly the river's intelligence
changed into the hysterics of monkeys
and the branches dripped ants
on my arms, which I stared at.
Things happen, human things.
I lay on my back, the sun forced its hand
down my throat, this was not the hard part,
this was private, I was a woman
and thus had permission, the howlers
fled, my child being only one morsel
for the corrupt ghosts that tear us asunder, one by one
the red hearts are shucked,
now it was my turn,
not by a poisoned dart
at two hundred English yards
is the raven brought down
but by eating an apricot
on which a flashlight battery
has leaked. HA!

So I come to my sister's house for two reasons:
to lament the death of my nephew,
and to prove I am sane.
By linking word to word, picture to picture
my black-as-the-raven spirit
plunges into the river
and climbs out on the opposite bank
an albino.

IO.

*She does women's work. The despair subsides. She knows she has the
special powers of song, and that the Dead desire her. Only very poor
persons continue their chores past nightfall.*

Red-cricket comes up and chirps,
knowing what it is like
toiling to scorn in the dark.
Its antennae wipe one another, "Why do you grieve
little woman, not so old, 'worn-stirring-stick'?"
I bring down the pestle
absently,
the old stars keep their distance from me
and from one another.
From under the constantly banged mortar
the millipede ripples.
The nightjars join me,
as do the treefrogs no eye has seen, human or ghost.
Blame sorcery or the Englishman's "fate."
The jawbones of skulls can trip you in the dark.
My sister rocks on her thighs. Soon she too
will shine like tourist-wood, the red-oil hand
dipped in porridge, even the thief's,
she will welcome,
anything to give her status and name.
But Mother could whistle
as well as a hunter, a man, could
sing the songs until the neighbors
leaned forward, absorbed. And she

taught me those things.
Though I am scoffed at, called chicken-men-chase-after-nightfall,
must sit after sunset grinding grain,
shaking the mealy-worms in the sieve,
some power, some arrogance, makes
the red-cricket approach, wiping its antennae,
scraping its underwings and letting
peep through the layers
its little earthworm-wet penis
to please me.

II.

*She cannot overcome the power of the men or the authority of the
sorcerer, or change the fates of the young girls embarking on lives of
abject servitude. But by singing the songs she can break the rules and
partly usurp the male role. Childless, husbandless, she accepts the fate
of the female seer and singer of songs. A "satisfied man"—euphemism
for a sorcerer, a man who is the opposite of satisfied.*

I have my double
in this world, this side of Death.
She knows what griefs narrow the needle.
Feed someone once and you are forever
the slave of their needs.
Mother, I did not write
the song-of-the-circumcision-of-the-girls,
when the hag intones,
"I come to you as a man, cold as a man,
otherwise I could not do this for you!"
A truth with a lie on its back.
We would not starve if the men did not hunt.
Our porridge would lack garnish, period.
The elephant meat is sweet and red,
but extra.
Even the hunters know they stalk mainly the magic,
the forest's alertness,
their status.
I envision those who fled the world into death

to avoid injury:
my daughter, my nephew, maybe even that prick
Ribs-showing.
Who is tidying up her vagina for him
as I jab this sharp stick in the yams?
Beauty is like breaking camp,
gone, circles of ash.
Already a bevy of girls, like fresh mushrooms,
smooth and sociable,
has sprung up.
And the locals have moved downstream of the model cattle farm
to exploit the diamond-bearing mud there.
Fat chance.
It was the sorcerer Spit-eyes who met my daughter
at the crossroads
and looked her up and down
the week before she died.
Against him I have no power
but this dirge for my nephew
in which I mix my own sorrows and threats.
Deaths are not separate but link up.
Though they call me chicken-in-the-dark,
any-man's-chicken,
I will sparkle and puff like a rooster,
that no "satisfied man" wring *my* neck.

This poem is indebted to the transcript of an oral poem by Ndaaya, a woman of Zaire, as it appears in *Leaf and Bone: African Praise Poems* by Judith Gleason, New York, Viking Press, 1980, and to Ms. Gleason's commentaries on African poems throughout her book.

Icy gravy,
that's my splendor.
Every bowl of icy gravy I remember.

I have seen the ladle
rise and fall
from the icy cradle.

And when I am really feeling
like the paper on the ceiling
icy gravy does the healing.

The dried up fly
on the sill between the panes
is my birthstone.

When I eat
icy gravy I'm complete:
feet and brain

make one full baby.
All completeness I can know
I partly owe to icy gravy.

When I die
and all my birthstones
come to see my soul congeal

write this on the box of bones:
Here lies one who ate his fill
Of icy gravy every meal.

§ "WHAT IS YOUR PREDICTION?"
"NO ONE WILL KNOW THE FUTURE."

I *will* love you.
And you will have no say in the matter.
You will be sitting reading.
I will step through the wall and take you by the ears.
Gold Latin will come out of your mouth.
Years will pass.
We will be old.
I will have loved you, against my nature,
no other being worthy,
thrown as I am on my own powers,
alone there.
And as we sit together reading you will say
"Did you *really* love me?"
And I will be terrified.

§ EMOTIONS

I.

Why did we evolve with EMOTIONS?
Does a brain "need" EMOTIONS?
Would we not have been more efficient and successful
    had we not developed
      EMOTIONS?
Is the EMOTIONAL a punishment?
Is suffering necessary?
Can reason suffer?
If we had no EMOTIONS would there be the "irrational"?
Isn't the statement "that is irrational" EMOTIONAL?
Is there a species which is completely rational
    but un EMOTIONAL?
Is the chimpanzee entirely EMOTIONAL?
Can a chimpanzee be reasoned with?
Can we be simultaneously rational and EMOTIONAL?
Why is the EMOTIONAL frequently irrational?
Why are the EMOTIONS divisible into separate "kinds"?
Is the division of the EMOTIONS into separate kinds
    a function of reason?
Can these questions be asked only of mammals?
Is the efficiency of the insect "rational"?
Is the increasing sophistication of the brain
    attributable to the dominance of reason
    or of EMOTION?
Is compassion an EMOTION?
Is the absence of compassion evidence of the lack of
    reason or the lack of EMOTION?
Do EMOTIONS hinder us?
Are we currently evolving more or fewer
    EMOTIONS?
Are EMOTIONS more primitive than reason?
Are reason and EMOTION divergent points
    on the cognitive spectrum
    like infrared and ultraviolet?
Are reason and EMOTION centers of patterns
    that are un-related,
    like yellowness and justice?
    Are the senses inherently EMOTIONAL?

Is seeing more rational than smelling?
Is memory an EMOTIONAL phenomenon?
Is the memory of having been rational
    EMOTIONAL?
Are all social structures attempts
    to regulate EMOTIONS?
Are EMOTIONS inherently dangerous?
Are some EMOTIONS more rational than others?
Are questions EMOTIONAL?
Are answers "rational"?
I wonder.

2.

Ocean, creation, accretion, emotion.
Creature, feature, teacher, reaches her station.
Frolic, symbolic, alcoholic, fierceness.
Ablution, contusion, confusion, diastolic.
Treason, formation, elation, confession, dysfunction.
Entity, clarity, mystery, scarcity, nearness.
Sanity, pity, pleasure, conjunction.
Erection, election, infection, reaches her treasure.
Initiate, aggravate, health, excitation.
Pattern, cistern, imitate, sight.
Seeing, aggrieving, masturbate, bastion.
Fashion, imply, ravenous, dry.
Illumined, emphatic, hieratic, ignite.
Passionate, intricate, active, align.
Actually, utterly, finally, hive.
Ornament, creamy, seamless, decried.
Zipped, focused, slippered, unsaid.
Fostered, upholstered, fingered, alive.

I met my enemy on the street today,
His hair (I was glad to notice) is gray
Now and his face soft and lumpy.
His two little boys were with him
(Against whom I have nothing—but pity)
And we traded our civilized
Insincerities while storming my brain
From every extremity
Was a shower of whitecold needles
That made his face in my Image
A bleeding dandelion seedpod.
We exchanged our enemy smiles
And parted. We were quite close
To the psychology of the gods.

Owl or dove, squeak of rat,
holsteins, wool lamb, lamp.
I am no shepherd. I am no shepherd.
Can't lead the spiders to water.
Or the vines from their vain dance.
The lace dress that once was a life
lives beyond human time now.
We dream her up. She is a dove,
or an owl.

Exaggeration has its price.
The rain ticks on the glass.
There's a law to all this. Down into
my mouth I let the mask-flesh slip.
All through the bible the fat dripped.
And the dead threw up on their towels.
Still she stayed: a dove, an owl.

The roman pigeon stood on sticks,
braiding the straw and pieces of wire
in the shit on the balcony outside
my room on the Via Condotti.
The cooing lighter than souls
beat up from the white dirt
of the flowerpots lighted all night
on the street of leathers below.
I walked down to the hotel bar for a beer.
The rough vulgar shepherds were there.
Cursing hatred, cursing love.
She was there too. On a stool at the bar.
Bosomed. Taloned. An owl of a dove.

§ SWEETMEAT

(after Davenport's Sappho)

God's gorgeous youngest daughter, Sweetmeat,
don't tease me with your flirting, fox,
confusing me with maybes, talking trash,
come to me as you did you-know-when,

leave your daddy's fancy condo for the streets
in your Firebird, come and get me,
the top down, your face a blur
in full warpaint, lipstick and eyeshadow,

like a stoned ghost.
In the alley, in the shadows, outside
the liquor store, it's all like Heaven
when I'm with you (no kidding), you make the others

just so many ugly sisters
batting their eyelashes, with your fine
apple-in-cold-water skin,
cruel and sweet, crush against me

and make me glad I was born.

The lemon,
and the lime
the apple,
and the peach
fall on black
death like bleach.

Sirs: I wrote to the Lord
of Letters. No answer.
It has been ten weeks.
That is plenty of time.
"My bleeding heart at least deserved an answer . . .
send me back my manuscripts . . .
I am an imbecile . . .
think of me what you will. . . ."
A. Artaud, somewhere in Europe.
Then the second flood came
the night we went to the opera.
It was wonderful. We walked up the aisle. We held hands.
For the first time in my life I had a reason to go on living
which was my reason, which no one had lent me.
Of course I need you.
Why else do you think I write this way?
A. Artaud, a photograph, 1930, his eyes
already as mad as a parrot's.
Europe completely Americanized in a twinkle.
Nothing left to say except Thank You Very Much.
Flood as slow as marble,
with an inner twinkle of quartz.
Then I took a job in the Ministry of Irrigation,
Alexandria, the Greek Sector,
and promoted the literary use of the demonic.
For thirty years I worked at my desk in the day
and at night wrote poems,
and died of throat cancer,
and that after an operation that took away my voice.
I should have taken precautions,
not talked until morning in the cafes
drinking Turkish coffee,
and come home, and rarely changed clothes,
and partially died in a straitjacket on a ship
halfway to Ireland.
That was a bitch of a lesson.
They accused me of trying to do myself harm. When
I told them it was *my* self

to destroy as I saw fit,
they did the buckles.
Well, they were afraid.
Of course I need you.
Why else do you think I send you these letters?
(1967)

A NOTE ABOUT THE AUTHOR

Stan Rice was associated for many years with San Francisco
State University, as assistant director of the Poetry Center,
and then as chairman of the Creative Writing Department.
He is the author of three earlier books of poems. He
received the Academy of American Poets Edgar Allan Poe
Award for the third of these, to acknowledge the
continuing achievement of a poet under forty-five. He now
lives in New Orleans.

A NOTE ON THE TYPE

The text of this book·was set in Sabon, a type face designed by Jan Tschichold (1902–1974), the well-known German typographer. Because it was designed in Frankfurt, Sabon was named for the famous Frankfurt type founder Jacques Sabon, who died in 1850 while manager of the Egenolff foundry.

Based loosely on the original designs of Claude Garamond (c. 1480–1561), Sabon is unique in that it was explicitly designed for hot-metal composition on both the Monotype and Linotype machines as well as for film composition.

Composition by Creative Graphics Inc.
Allentown, Pennsylvania
Printed and bound by Fairfield Graphics,
Fairfield, Pennsylvania
Designed by Harry Ford